Vahni Capildeo was born and educated in Trinidad and holds a DPhil in Old Norse from Christ Church, Oxford. Landscape, language and memory inform her poetry and prose, notably those of Caribbean, Indian diaspora, Icelandic, Scottish and Northern cultures. She has worked in academia; for the Commonwealth Foundation; at the Oxford English Dictionary; and as a volunteer with Oxfam and Rape Crisis. As Judith E. Wilson Poetry Fellow 2014 at the University of Cambridge, she developed approaches to poetry through collaborative and immersive events. The Harper-Wood Studentship (2015) at St John's College, Cambridge, will see her exploring similar collaborations abroad.

Vahni Capildeo

Measures of Expatriation

CARCANET

First published in Great Britain in 2016
by Carcanet Press Limited
Alliance House, 30 Cross Street,
Manchester, M2 7AQ
www.carcanet.co.uk

Cover photograph by Elspeth Duncan,
reproduced with kind permission.

Typeset by LA in Arnhem Pro. A CIP
catalogue record for this book is
available from the British Library,
ISBN 9781784101688

The publisher acknowledges financial
assistance from Arts Council England.

Supported using public funding by

**ARTS COUNCIL
ENGLAND**

MIX
Paper from
responsible sources
FSC
www.fsc.org   FSC® C014540

Contents

V

VI

VII

for Jeremy Noel-Tod
Eadig bið se þe eaþmod leofaþ

Measures of Expatriation — I

Handfast

for K. M. Grant

She is away.
The feathers in my eye spoke outwards.
She is the accident that happens.
The sun bursts hazel on my shoulders.
She is the point of any sky.

Come here, here, here:
if it's a tree you'd sulk in, I am pine;
if earth, I'm risen terracotta;
if it's all to air you'd turn, turn to me.
You are flying inside me.

Seventy times her weight,
I stand fast.
My hand is blunt and steady.
She is fierce and sure:
lands, scores, punctures the gloveskin.

And why I asked
for spirals stitched where she might perch:
fjord blue, holm green, scarlet, sand,
like her bloodline, Iceland to Arabia:
because her hooded world's my hand –

The tears curled from the cattle's eyes, their horns curled back, their coats curled like frost-ferns on windshields or the hair on the heads of Sikandar's soldiers. Two of my grandfather's sons, when he knew he was dying, took him from his bed. They supported him out the doorway so he could say goodbye to his favourite cattle. The cattle wept. They knew him. They are not like cattle here. They live among the household and on the hills, which are very green, and they eat good food, the same food as the household, cut-up pieces of leftover chapatti.

You do not get stories like that in books. I am telling you because you only have things to read. Whenever anybody tried to make me read a book or anything, I would fall asleep; my head would just drop.

What is the use of reading books? What can you do after that but get an office job? Do my friends who stayed at school earn as much as me? They all have office jobs; could they do a job like mine? Could they slaughter for seventy hours without getting tired or needing to sleep?

It was hard at first. I used to dream the cattle. They would come to me with big eyes, like mothers and sisters. After a few weeks, they stopped coming to me in dreams. After about five years, I stopped feeling tired: I do not need to sleep. We do three or four thousand a day in Birmingham, only a thousand a night in Lancaster.

Tonight I am going to Lancaster. I will talk to you until Lancaster. Where are you from? You are lying on me. No, where are your parents from? Are you lying on me? I came here as a teenager, and at once they tried making me read. How old are you? Why do you only have things to read? I am sorry I am talking to you. You have brought things you want to read. Beautiful reader, what is your name?

You can feel the quality of the meat in the animal when it is alive: the way its skin fits on its flesh. You can feel the quality of life in the meat. The cattle here are not good. They inject them. Their flesh is ahhh.

Look, look how beautiful. I will show you pictures of the place. Look, it is very green.

O Love, that fire and darkness should be mix'd,
Or to thy triumphs such strange torments fix'd!
– John Donne, Elegy XIII

A northern street: the temperature of the ungovernable. The proud
hooded stride. The skill to add up stone: cold – outlasting. The wealth
of the land: stone. Kindness: the harsh kind. For each question, a
better question. For each better question, one answer. For each good
question – that'll do. Not fussed.

I walk the hollow walk: loving more than loved; moved, scarce more
than moving.

and also

In the south of this country, five times I have attended the celebra-
tions that they hold in the dark of the year. Many centuries ago, there
was a man whose name was Guy, or Guido. He practised a different,
competing version of the national religion. He tried to explode an
important government site. These buildings are still in use. You can
visit the place, which is on the river. Some of the children who ask for
money on British streets are simply trying to fund their construction
of effigies of this hate figure, whose burning on public and domestic
pyres on the so-called 'Bonfire Night' (5 November) has become a pop-
ular ritual. Fireworks are let off; it is legal to purchase them for your
own festivities.

no join

A northern street, uphill. It branches, like – a Y, a peace sign, water
coursing round an outcrop; like – part of the net of a tree; like – It
branches in two. Upon the slope held between the branches stands a
sooty church, now in use as a nightclub. This pale and brisk morning
glances on the metal railings.

Who is he?
Nobody.
Who is he, between the fence and lamp post?
Nobody. A hat stuck on the railing, abandoned by a tidy drunk. A
feeble visual joke. Nobody's head, nobody's, supports a hat drooped
at that angle.

It is a guy. A Guy Fawkes guy. The students left him there: lad for the
burning: unreal, it has to be unreal. Check out this guy.

I have to cross the road, so I do.

The ordinary-looking foot is wedged between the base of the fence
and the lamp post. The left arm, bent at the elbow, has been tucked
deep into the jacket pocket, toneless. It is not a bad face. The eye is

the pity of it: tender lids tightened into a crescent, as happens with mortally wounded birds; infolding, no longer able to yield, a turning inwards of the ability to light up.

I put my hand into my pocket, for my phone.

It is not necessary.

Pale and brisk as this morning, the police car slides into my peripheral vision.

and also

A street in Trinidad: the soft, brown 'ground doves' have the same manners as the pedestrians. Unhurried, they traipse along in front of cars. Why did the ground dove cross the road? I don't know, but it's certainly taking its time.

The exception came plummeting out of the recessive sky, into the back yard's concrete rain gutter. Had a neighbourhood boy felled it inexpertly? Had the ecstatic efficiency of its heart thumped to a stop? It lay there, the softness, and would not, could not bestir itself.

The child strewed it with yellow and scarlet wild lantana flowers, thinking of burial, accustomed to cremation; feeling a sudden fear. The parents took it all away.

And when the dove was gone, another came plummeting the same way; the riddle repeated – to be moved, moving, and never to move. Love or some other force was identical in the equation.

no join

We brought few friends home who were not already part of at least a two-generation family circle. We brought few friends home. This time my brother had introduced a soft and brown and tallish young man in his early twenties, who weighed not much more than a hundred pounds. By historical pattern, not personal choice, in our secular Hindu household, this was the first Muslim friend our age.

Perhaps it has changed; but non-Indo-Caribbeans used not to be aware that 'Ali' and 'Mohammed' are not 'Indian' names. And in that unawareness they are linguistically wrong, but more profoundly right: for our ancestors brought over a shared Indian village culture, over a century before the creation of Pakistan in the Indus area made such a difference. And in that Trinidad remote from Trinidad's Trinidad, and nonetheless most mixed and Trinidadian, a lunatic reverberation was set up by the 1947 Partition – some third-generation immigrant families briefly fought according to the lines of what had not been a division. In lands far away, current events were indirectly regenerating or inventing this part of Trinidad's past also. By 1990, we knew that there must be some difference.

We sat on the nice imported sofa with the delicate novel unicorn visitant who looked just like us.

All over the island, every evening just before seven, telephone calls were wound down, fires turned low beneath pots, and families converged on the television set to listen to the news headlines: a link with the greater world. Nothing was expected to happen.

A square, reliable face showed up.

'The liberation of Kuwait has begun.'

The look of devastation and betrayal on our guest's face was like nothing I could have imagined seeing. An outline seemed to be sitting in his place, while the person who had occupied that outline crumbled.

Why? Televised missile fireworks were going off, white and purple. What had so upset him?

I tried to see with his eyes. Brownskinned people with strong features and children of adorable gravity were being killed from the air; and en masse they looked more like us than anyone else on television, local or international, in those days. My insides flipped. People who looked like they could be family were being killed from the air.

We are not evolved to cope with aerial threats. To witness the spectacle of bombing is to feel guilty and due to be wiped out; for all our gods inhabit the heavens, and to be safe our earliest kind might have taken to the trees, where only the gods could smite them. To be bombed is to be smitten by the wrath of a Deity not to be located and not in our image. To ascend into Heaven becomes profoundly and secretly inconceivable; for the borders of the heavens are guarded with fire.

Was this what our friend was seeing? The starring roles in war, in our young memories, hitherto had been for people who did not look like us. Or was he seeing war upon his religion?

From now on, anyway, in the world's play of representations of the living, we would look more like the killed. We would resemble – like it or not – anti-advertisements for flourishing societies; which is perhaps why people on the street in the south of England have told me that they have no money, or have offered me money, when I have said nothing or when I was about to ask for directions and certainly have not had a guy to burn.

Our soft brown young man sat, and sat, until he could get himself home.

no join

no join

no join

and also

like

like

like

Speech ~ ~ ~ Silence

It is easier to touch a shape of air than to speak to you.

Here they call it *thinking too much*. Thought has nothing to do with it. The moment of encounter between myself and another; the encounter-before-crossing; the moment of encounter-about-to-become event (long scratch of glass on glass, mutual crystal transfer): *too much.*

How too much? The instantaneousness with which a world opens within me and I am sightless, tremulous, rooted to the spot before whomsoever-it-must-be-and-you-alone:
> Another sky, washing out and out, filled with birds creating and obeying a summons, an arc: the percussive seagull crying an ocean somewhere; the golden hardwood doors of eagle wings slamming a warning to walkers to flatten their path away from the nest at the peak; the unsettling flock of smaller birds intimating the existence of a gable, a tower, spare masonry: caught up in the sense of habitual, never-accustomed flight (yours, mine) I am silent before you (everything) and the adorable mispronunciations of names.

The creation of this inner world (that expands into the outer, carries all before it) destroys the instant of encounter, making an almost immeasurably small but acutely perceptible interval; the neat rip of an abyss in which eyes wander or are dropped, voices falter or rise headlong, and the body rearranges itself into a perhaps less than social attitude:
> Desert heat pushes you back, even before the metallic etiquette of polite words applies itself and seals up your tender tentative of speech; green and moist blossoming begins to crack up the arch stonework of greeting and the unique transformation of love lays out a courtyard for friendship that perhaps wanted a lesser space, perhaps wanted only a bench in the shade, perhaps has become an exile beyond welcome who turns away bewildered by plenitude.

But what do they see?
> Here in my adult life I have stood outside a community doorway, a decade ago, having knocked and about to exit, dressed in martial arts white, and been asked by a woman very little my senior with a voice of blankets, *Who do you belong to?*, for she saw a foreign child. Here in my family life I have sat within a commercial doorway, in the decade previous, ensconced with my shopping bags in the waiting area, wearing purple silk and expecting my mother's arrival, and

been told by a bob-haired woman with a voice of posters, *I'm sorry, I haven't got anything,* for she saw a beggar.

It is easier to touch a shape of air than to speak to you.

I have seen the eyes of a woman fill entirely with black (cornea and iris), not the eyeholes of a mask but the active blackness of a surge in the universe inimical to the development of life.

I have seen the eyes of a man fill entirely with blue (cornea and iris), not a lake into which to step but lapis lazuli, the animate statue of a jackal elevated to Egyptian godhood bringing in judgment on the human soul before him.

I have seen the eyes of a boy whirl like a Chinese dragon's and on another occasion seen the woman who fostered a strenuous, undeclared love of him make articulate conversation in his absence about something not-him while she herself seemed to be dissolving dissolving dissolving like a round of pearls dropped one by one into a cup of expensive, acidic drink.

It is easier to touch a shape of air than to speak to you ~ ~ ~ snail balanced on a box hedge reaching for a pink rose petal shed by force of rain and barely at any distance from the singing nerves, the brown thorns.

Here you are.

Mercy and Estrangement

His heart hurtling towards me
I not caring to catch it
it turns into a bird, turns:
a scavenger bird lightfoot
alights on foam, contests white
as silver tilts white, silver
as refuse seams silver, gawks,
jinks, is radiated by charts
charted inly: magnetic,
unhoming because transformed.
A rill and jitter brought me
 – birdform, my heart – to the park
where state translators, laid off,
sat sad for their hospitals,
prisons and schools. Laws whistled
infixes between trained ears.
And at our conference,
so many equivalents
for *gracias* and *Verfremdung*,
easy change amongst false friends.

A Personal Dog

for Vivek Narayanan

it isn't matter
isn't doesn't matter
does it compared
with what shan't
have known your
lines are all
lines of approach
this dog's eyelids
this delhi dog's
intentional eyelids, this
doorway dog, this
dog fellating beggars
delhi exuding matter
nictitation cannot extrude
America to england
the third nictitating
poetry is over
eyelid cannot eject
America to england
large foreign bodies
poetry is over
over and out
surgery rarely happens
over and ours
dogs aren't loved
over here, here!
sufficiently foreign bodies
remain requiring incision
mind yourself it
happened before you
as you go
you're nothing cold
sunshine practised apprehension

Too Solid Flesh

for Anu Lakhan

Cross the road and you can walk south into an urban space that looks immemorial. Aston's Eyot is the site of a nineteenth-century midden; an old dump. The refuse heated up underground. Apple cores and pear seeds and walnut kernels matured into a wilderness too hybridized for names. Sprays of blackberries and rosehips arch red and black; sloes add notes of steely blue; a willow grows askant a brook. Other walkers are seldom met or heard. There are trodden paths but also many turnings.

She four-thousand-miles-away-across-the-ocean hasn't been herself lately. She hermits more and more. She would have liked the walk. Now I am home for another Saturday night...
'My thoughts have turned to green leaves.'
'Well, that's better than sorrow. I'm so tired of living in this nameless sadness, even I am bored by myself.'
'Do you keep a diary? A document of marvellous and total self-obsession?'
She feels like an invalid of centuries past, to be rolled out into the sun. Who would push the chair? A lithe and grateful illiterate youth?
'A brilliant lavender and lace parasol-carrying creature with an air of reckless innocence...'

She four-thousand-miles-away-across-the-ocean has often felt, as have many others, that she is disconnected from her corporeal self. I am feeling out of touch with my body: it feels like something I have been given to look after. When I bathe I feel that I am washing it, not that I am bathing. She likes that I speak of it as being a thing I take care of, like a costume or a small animal.
How do I take care of it? Why is it not mine? Might a description get me closer to making it mine, or at least an understanding of why I am at odds with it?
She-who-hermits-more-and-more offers a description: leaning over a claw-footed tub, body costume in hand, I may gently soap and groom it... bathe it in milk and rose petals... take delicate brushes to it... do I? For it needs to understand not what it doesn't have but what it needs.
She desires me to immerse myself in the hows and whys.

The howls and wiles!
It wants things.
It is an idiot child.
It understandeth not that there is no store of warmth.
It has forgotten thirst.
A reminder to myself: water, at least every three hours. A reminder from

myself: nudity, between clothing it at least twice a day. A reminder of
myself: carefulness, up and down the steep expressionist stairs.

It wakes expectant. The look of ceiling meets its eye, or the look of cur-
tain. Expectancy is worst.

A reminder, not to expect?

No. Clinging helplessly to its capabilities, ever hopeful of change, it
issues reminders that are first cousin to cravings.

For her, in the sun perhaps; certainly elsewhere; like me, insufficiently
solid; for her, this description, a near-total avoidance of the one with
which I was tasked.

Because I am superstitious, I am stringing a series of lights between
this and anything else that happens.

★

It was inconceivable to me that there had been nothing on the land in
the residential area of Port of Spain where my family's house was built,
though I knew the construction date was in 1971, and some of the build-
ing materials from the quarry my grandfather owned; thereby his ill
elder son and unarranged daughter-in-law were enabled to hide respect-
ably and save face for the family. There is no such thing as nothing.

Our storybooks were English and children in them ran around thou-
sand-year-old castles or two-hundred-year-old vicarages; our myths
were Hindu and we were encouraged to imagine many civilizations in
a universe cyclically created and destroyed; and our island geography,
we were told, had been Arawak and Carib.

The land sloped down, just over a quarter of an acre of it. There
were mostly well-behaved trees and one frightening one, but there
was also somehow the feeling of where trees had been. I do not mean
stumps or even irregularities in the ground. There was more to this
than the suggestion of seeding patterns of kush grass and razor grass,
windflowers, lily spathes and snake plants. A child not allowed, for all
sorts of reasons, to play much with other children started to know the
nameless lilac trumpets, no bigger than two millimetres, that never
did figure in textbooks; the partly concreted-over gap into unfathoma-
ble dark, possibly created by earthquake or earlier watercourses, which
the grown-ups placed stones in front of only to find the stones moved
away just enough to let something muscular through; and the patches
of brooding that you might explain by the humidity of a present micro-
climate, but which I took to be the past knotting up of fibres into the
concentration of a tree.

It was indoors, just inside the threshold of my bedroom, that I dreamt
the woman who had tan yellow skin and a shearing rag of silk for hair.
She was not the unwrapped mummy from the dead-house museums

abroad. She was not quite my aunt's maid, who was over here from South America and was the first 'Arawak' I thought I had ever seen, since we were mis-taught that ours were extinct from ancient conflicts. She was more like that, though; yes, indigenous, a category scarcely acknowledged in Trinidad, to which people have been waves. She smiled at me and her smile went up toothily at the corners, because her flesh no longer covered skull.

'I'm as solid as you are,' she said loudly and tonguelessly. Her arms extended themselves and my upper arms were grasped hard between the elbow and shoulder. 'I'm as solid as you are.'

I knew she could not be.

'I'm solid as you are.'

But I was alive, and she was not. I broke free and woke up. I arrayed my mind with ferocity and identified a day.

★

It should be early evening. Can you see the individual flames, and the bronze tiger?

Janaki is tall. When she opened the wardrobe and I saw the array of clothes, it seemed right. There is stateliness in her modesty. The formal garments glistering there matched her presence almost weight for weight. She is pure gold.

A statue, moving: does that call up a nightmare scene? Why? A statue, moving: can that instil a sense of peace? It is, is so. Each gesture it makes should be made with consideration: otherwise it risks breaking itself or crushing that which it would reach or touch. Respecting its own range of possible movements, it would respect your space. If it made an approach, it could never be appropriate. It could only approximate you, so wearily, as only stone can be weary, for its way of breathing is to lose itself: each micropore exhales dust in a tiny brightening of the air, and with each exhalation the stone is less.

I read today of the man in his early forties pierced to death by metal as he dismantled a bridge under government orders.

There are inevitabilities that need not have become inevitable had there been the difference made by thought.

A statue, moving: pure matter so considered as to have identity with pure thought? Pure is a strange word.

Anyway, it took both hands for me to lift one of those garments on its wooden hanger. I imagined her inhabiting it, thin-backed, barefoot and gracious in mud or on tiles in that territory where a dream of the village East washes through into somewhere western, momentarily eroding the reality of both, sometimes leaving permanent alterations in its wake; somewhere like Trinidad, so Indian even if not considered so, so Western even if not called so, thumbnail of the Americas, immigrant blood opal at its base.

The weight of it I couldn't bear though I loved her for wanting to lend it to me. I gave up. I was the ghost.

The need to acquire weight followed me north and overseas. Imagine a pointilliste vision given an order of dismissal: the dots of colour that vibrate until the eye interlinks them and learns the trick of making sense of the person or the landscape depicted, these dots would obediently dance apart, disperse, making image into worse than nonsense, hurting the eye that tries to focus into questing after a scattering in which each particle is adamantine uncollectable. Being looked at, I was that unmade image, that hurt in return.

People who talked to me were unable to keep their countenance. I was not as dense as the object would need to be for them to focus on it. Their question, 'Where is she from?' in my very presence became, 'Where is she?'

I had the unfortunate effect of making segments of their heads disappear. These did not always reappear positioned correctly. This effect was deathlike in that nobody was immune. So you will better understand that, I shall tell you about the Armed Forces man. He had the kindness to ignore the others at the dinner table, in order to explain to me how I might acquire density: essentially, I was the same as any woman, if we could put aside the intellect. Abruptly, he took on the aspect of a pegged grapefruit of which one quarter had been eaten. His head not only disappeared; it also came apart.

The Armed Forces man's voice continued to make itself heard. Others around the table nodded vigorous support of his views. Now all of them were missing something. A solid and crystalline seam of absence scarred them from temple to jawbone. I searched in vain for any faces. Voice kept tilting out of voids. I got up and left the table in some distress.

I had not yet decided to abandon the scene, so I exited to the bathroom, where iridescent lights were strung across the bathtub and there was no shower and no soap. I looked in the mirror and did not see myself, which brought some comfort. A classic moment had enveloped me. The same had happened to Vidia Naipaul's father; but in his time, non-being brought with it horror and insult. I could and did wait. That I was a trick of the light, I accepted. Failing to pull myself together, I left the party without embarrassment, indeed without a proper farewell, and started walking.

The knife crime boys were not at the end of the road that day. At the corner I passed a woman pushing a pram. She was chatting to another woman, who carried a bag of shopping. They were not as old as I am. More had happened around their eyes. They seemed to see and not see me. Their aura of sociability expanded, spreading with a faint juddering as they drew near. They walked me off the pavement into the gutter.

I was too horrified to say 'Excuse me'. The hands in charge of the baby carriage had no wrists. A seam of void extended beyond the sleeves. No cross-section of bone and pulsing bluecrimson evidenced itself. Just solidity again, palpable absence. The same apparent chasm joined the set of fingers grasping the plastic shopping bag to the pinkish banister of arm. The women moved like a staircase next to a lift shaft down which I and my kind dropped.

Reading, a sedentary occupation except on places like the London train, where tickets are sold after the last seat is gone, and the area of corridor between First Class and standard class carriages is much coveted by those who can find floor early enough to settle down with a book until forced upright by the briefcased, backpacked, mobile telephone users... Reading could fix me. It could be a way to acquire weight. Consider the women in academic posts, whose faces are keener than normal and who rise like bells from an ever widening base. I have seen one such white-stockinged and long-skirted in the south-west, and dared not wonder how long it would take for her legs to meld together into one. Then she would ring out and trundle towards the apex of a career, wild for the literature that has been written, for no more need be written, for literature is the province of the dead, and how can I have something to add to it? To the bells that clamour over the greening inscriptions, I can but ghost the living past...

I opened a book and a mango fell out. I opened another, and another mango fell out. These were newly published books: fresh leaves.

Woman doth not live by mango alone. Was there more goodness in volumes of essays or in novels? Were specialist shops and second-hand departments a good bet in the search for sustenance?

After a couple of weeks or perhaps ten or twelve years, with something like desperation I totalled the yield, excluding mangos:

2 quarts desiccated coconut

1 breadfruit

Half a yam

A grain of salt

A grain of match

A piece of camphor

1 measure sweet (maraschino)

10 measures sour (lime)

100 measures strong (rum)

1 tin condensed milk (for sandwiches)

1 tin condensed milk (for tea)

5 enamel cups

Cream crackers

Curried shrimp

A 1950s bookmark with a school crest defaced with the motto *Sufficient unto the dhal is the weevil thereof* (fountain pen, italic)

(I did not buy the book that had the tablecloth)

(The coal pot presumably had been removed by the police after he was found to have succumbed to carbon monoxide poisoning)

This left over a hundred and seventy mangos, despite the careful selection process.

'I do not know what to do with all these mangos.'

'Take them to market,' said the agent with half a face.

'The same ones?'

'You were glad enough to find them, weren't you?' he said, answerably.

Mine is one of the few corners of the city not assailed by pigeons. On my way to buy the weightiest bread I could, I noticed the absence of pigeons; for the food of many peoples was strewn or for sale along the pavements. A lot of reading must have been going on, if even a few of these nostalgic, often faintly toxic fruits had fallen from the leaves of books. A volatile, ratty iridescence of pigeons would have flocked towards such riches in Oxford city centre, but there are seldom such spills between the spires; perhaps nobody reads there at all, or perhaps the opening of books is no such unsealing.

A woman friend with a head full of music and hips like a cello... solider than I am... once met me in the market square among those urbocentric pigeons, her face phosphorescent with fear. That was when I began finding out how widespread pigeon phobia is in the south of England; as inconvenient in its way as the well-diagnosed lizard phobia in the Caribbean.

How different the child with bronze fluff for hair who had laughed in the streets of Florence as he went towards the pigeons and stamped. Again and again he stamped, his face a forum for the mingling of cruelty and glee. The birds, stupid with alarm, went and settled, went and settled, not seeming to identify an attacker, unable to deal with the repeated fact that they could not stay in what they felt to be their place. He was an infant Perseus. He was cause; the rest of the world, effect. He impressed me as much as that other Perseus, bronze all through and smiling slenderly but solidly in the Piazza, the head of the Medusa in his hand.

Medusa's beautiful, wise serpentine head was cut off because she paralyzed people who looked at her. Was that it, or did people fear being seen through by her? Could they not bear to be known? Not by her, not as she could know. Crying paralysis, they stopped themselves in the presence of an amoral scrutiny in which everything is as it is, not as anyone would have it be, and the intricate is simple. Medusa's head was co-opted as a weapon, to be brought out of the man's bag when enemies needed to be stopped. Was this change of use good or bad or neither? One thing for sure: her quality of living contemplation had ceased to be in the possession of a female form moving with the constancy of the living. It had been made deathly, after being marked for death.

Bronze was ringing and serpents twirling somewhere in the past's past as I turned the corner.

I was solider than the girl behind the counter of the shop. She had a saline pallor like a washed rind cheese. The shelves were clean, but darkness clustered like flies; not darkness that one could see... it made the space between the wrappers of untranslated s/z sweets heavy with something yet more adaptable than shadow. The bread there was cheap and good, and I needed to acquire weight. If I met her eyes during our transaction, she too might solidify some more. This would benefit the neighbourhood. A slice of air circulating among the merchandise was clearly another customer who had disappeared altogether on seeing me in the wrong pigeonhole. (This shop was without salt fish or mangos.) The loaf, chock full of seeds, was the right size for a one-person household.

I took pleasure in the quietening of the street. A laugh, here and there, closed a shutter of air on the temporary private room of a pavement hello or goodbye. Light thickened. The small, dense grains opened strange flavours to the inside of my mouth. Changes were occurring in what my mind could visually process. Twilight was general throughout my apartment. A plain spread wide in my imagination. The scene constructed itself as I saw less and less of my actual surroundings. Terror and relief came at the moment of realization. Greyish green and dark brown, the almost-black of a cold field, and hair tossing in the abandonment of earth; pale limbs, shaped and furred similar to those I had known; and recent roots, shallow, hard at work, drawing out of the soil their nourishment from the uncountable breaking down of human beings into scandalously lamentable flesh. I saw the sprouting and greening of the plain, and the sheaves ripening towards harvest. The bread that was to have made me solid had undone itself and nearly undone me. I finished the meal. I could not finish the loaf. It was a hungry thing. There was too much time in it.

The glass overcoat was manufactured, if not developed, in that country where the grains of the loaf had grown. The glass overcoat gave automatic density. It was cast in one, seamless, except for tiny bubbling within the glass, like you get in marbles. Scratch-resistant and shatterproof, it was admittedly chill; less so to the wearer, who felt insulated by the build-up of body heat; felt, if anything, more flexible, within the range of movement that did remain possible. The people in glass overcoats spent a lot of time in transit. The main drawbacks to contact with others were evident. The smudges from everyday wear translated to rainbows. These were not so much a problem as was the gritty rain of that climate. This style of garment is out of fashion and no longer exported. Dubiously collectable, some turn up second-hand in England. Buying one and wearing it would show a real investment in... something.

The loneliness of the body is utterly different from the loneliness of the mind. Ready to race ahead, the mind is impatient when the body, untouched by anyone day after day, begins to shiver as bedtime draws near. The hands catch and hurt when undoing a button. They refuse to deal with the edge of the book, which tumbles to the floor, leaves flying. This shiver is not a thing of the surface. It is a shuddering from within, as if cold breaks out on the skin from a heart splintered into a rose of frost. Then the weightlessness of the bed must be resisted. It wants to assume the body. A wind of separateness drives at the outline of each fold and bend battered by ice. Sleep will not take under these conditions. A summer that dries out the linens within hours has no effect on the ague of isolation. A layer of black wool has to be worn at night-time in the hottest month of the year. The being practised in isolation not reconciling itself to the exercise in cruelty that is dream... It wakes warm and looks about, the body ready for a round of greetings. The mind knowing otherwise, ordering the smile wiped off the face, the tender weakness in the fingers to tense up, wakes a little annoyed at the insistence with which it is tipped into disappointment, having nothing to do but begin in silence and space, meeting only its own demands, without refreshment from a contradictory presence.

The scission, when I finished losing my body, was in January. Christmas was just past and I was due to travel up to Scotland for Hogmanay, so it was still the Old Year, the turn of winter over the calendar, when the high fever set in. I was invited to come north anyway, and be looked after; but I was not strong enough to deposit my temperature on the train and carry my germs across the Border.

I had been aware of greater tiredness than normal, but what is normal? Winter in Oxford was a scant pause for the trees that minded their own business and continued more or less strenuously to branch and bud. A layer of coconut frosting on the ground looked more like a birthday cake than serious weather, and disappeared faster.

So, this winter was not normal. The tall nineteenth-century windows that let in light from the south and west were filled with blackness in between falling snow. The snow fell, and settled, and went on falling. The snow settled, and did not melt, and more snow fell. A small white dog could have been buried in the amounts that drifted up around the annexe door. Twigs were coated to several times their thickness. The roofs of the next door pub and its add-on buildings could have been any shape under their pitiless cover. At whatever hour that I looked out, there were the lines and monuments of this winter's victory; and those were many hours.

For my tiredness was not normal. Overnight the skin of my face blistered and began to peel off like paint on a badly neglected wall. I had no thermometer. Was this fever? Morning after morning my lips, stuck together with dryness, needed lotion rubbed in to them before they would open and I could drink water. They cracked deeply and widely at the corners, visible slits as if made by a letter-opener, and bled as I took the first sips. I dabbed with a tissue, and saw scarlet. The cracks blistered but would not fill up with flesh or cover over with scab. The reasons I did not immediately ring the doctor are not to be told here; suffice it to say that I was too accustomed to people who varied between unseeing and unseen.

I creamed my lips and watched the winter. I became frightened only when the lead box installed itself in my rib cage: walking from the bedroom to the kitchen necessitated a stop on the sofa, and lifting a glass brought on hyperventilation.

Let these procedures not be questioned.

I visited the official website. The website diagnosed me with official swine flu. No tests would be done. I took the number I was issued, and knew it was pointless to call my doctor, for I could not get myself to that location. The official website informed me that everyone ill in Britain needed a 'flu friend', who would collect their medication. I rang a few acquaintants who might have stayed at home during the festive season. Their mobiles connected to differently pitched signals: international ones: before switching to answerphone. The woman in the flat above me had gone away. As usual, footsteps or creaky boards sounded in her empty flat; they were of no use. No post was being delivered through the snow, so there was no point looking for a pileup on the stairs that might tell me nobody had been in at all. I listened out. The great emptiness assured me that this house, divided into flats, was holding itself in during the snow. I was its breathing.

The official website directed me to the so-called Primary Care Trust. Relieved to see they were located in my neighbourhood, I rang. Soon antibiotics would drop through the brass flap; I would wander germily down the stairs, making rest stops when the lead box was awkward, and wander back up to start waging internal war against the infection. The person who answered the phone had an audible conversation with his colleague. *If she doesn't have a number and she hasn't spoken to her GP we don't have to give her the Tamiflu.* I gave the number several times, to two people, in the course of a few minutes. Each time, they seemed not to remember that I had consulted the website and given them an official number. I pushed back memories of Passport Control, and the memorable twenty minutes when I reiterate where I live or where I was born and the blandness of my desired voyaging... the classical music of the wrong origin; twenty minutes is long enough to perform some concertos. The Primary Care Trust would call me back.

The woman on the other end of the phone raised her voice and began a patter like a fishmonger desperate to move on her rotting wares and raise enough money to cover her husband's rum habit. *I had to have family; friends; co-workers; neighbours...?* You seem to have difficulty in understanding that someone might be alone at Christmas. *There must be someone...!* Only a friend, one of those truly dear friends who nonetheless are seen fewer than five times a year, in another village, expecting a second child, living with her toddler... exactly the Flu Friend to brave the House of Plague... *Well, if she's pregnant the child can't be* that *small!...* I realized that she had elicited a biography from me: of immigration, a broken relationship and unemployment: and an analysis, of how doors close on English houses during their holidays. The lead box was pressing closer to the surface of my chest. I raised my voice in turn and dehumanized the woman and rang off, and fell asleep with the effort of it. I woke to the doorbell. The reluctant health worker walked up a couple of stairs and extended her arm like a kindergarten flag waver at a national parade. I smiled infectiously at her and started down the stairs. With undisguised horror she thrust the tiny packet in its oversized envelope towards me, and fled.

Let these procedures not be questioned.

By this time I was not solid at all. I had the colours of Snow White: lips as red as blood (but in the wrong way); sky and hair black as ebony; and the slant of descending white to look at. What was inside, what was outside? I stopped trying to contact anyone, and found it would be two weeks or more before anyone would contact the childless, no-news nowherian. In those days something changed.

This was the first spring of disconnection.

So why not you and I... a music-box dusting itself off as its ballerina figurine twirls... Some melody played itself in previous springs, as pollen blew and temperate colours reasserted themselves waxily, waterishly, pink and white; the external and internal flickered up again, *always...*

This year I knew that had been youth. Spring would not come again with a sense of oneness. It was not in my future to soften and burgeon. The young kangaroo mothers and grim boyish lovers and ice-cream-on-a-stick screaming mess of children, the leafmeal and paper wrapper litter, swirled together, adhered to railings and bus stop signs, washed up again and toppled and proceeded to paint the city with an impression of life.

The hearts of the roses outside the Botanic Garden were an embarrassment of potential. The depth, the disclosure... Out of rhythm with the natural process, I became gentler with old people and thought about soldiers, whether for them spring had elements of homecoming.

The sun is so bright, the eye is a blackboard. The car approaching the crossroads slows down. Four walls of shimmering air are too much for the mind's eye. It perceives and makes memories of what it sees as if sitting in a cool classroom. A woman in white is waiting to cross the East Oxford road. She flutters. Her silhouette, instantly recognizable, feels extra familiar; her clothing is old-fashioned North Indian.

So much of cloth. An older woman's voice whispers disapproval in my ear. Why so much of cloth, when dresses would not be frowned on by the guardians of good behaviour? My grandmother's generation was already permitted to wear colonial-export challis cotton or georgette print, fastened with covered buttons like those on living room furniture. The knees would not quite be exposed. The uncovered legs might be sturdy, twentieth-century varicose originals of the limbs adored in bronze or sandstone by pre-Christian-era sculptors. The uncovered legs might be spindly, kin to those that bend again and again among the leaves of some labour-intensive crop on its way towards the airtight hold of a fragrant destiny. The partly razored legs might be sleek with cocoa butter or coconut oil, rubbed in by the hands of grandchildren who learn the mysteries of pain and age from the question-command, 'Come and rub your Ajee's legs!'

If you see the pictures like Auntie Sati had – you remember the batik pictures? – we never covered ourselves up. Covering ourselves up, that is a new thing. Maybe it is a Muslim thing, maybe it is a Western thing. Those women in the pictures, some of them are not even wearing a choli. They tie their sari across their bare chest. I do not know whether what the older voice says is true.

Widow: the white drapery identifies the woman poised at the kerbside. White-is-the-colour-of-brides-black-is-the-colour-of-mourning: *no*. Dissonant and spectral associations have to be pushed away when I sit in a church whose stony atmosphere is fertilized by the overspilling of satin and orchids and tears of joy as the bride navigates the aisle. The strong florals are overlaid by those of a tropical night and the cool striking up under my feet seems to strike up more directly. Sitting in church in the afternoon, facing a crucifix, I am standing barefoot in a marble courtyard in the dark, the Dancing Siva at my back, the Kali shrine still to be built. A row of women assembles itself on foldup metal chairs. They are in white drapery and look so much alike, whited out in widowhood, that I embrace my great-aunt, taking her for my grandmother.

Because I am superstitious, I am stringing a series of lights here once more.

★

'Black,' my mother says darkly, 'is a colour of joy.' Kali is black. Black contains all the colours; it is ultimate colour.

Can you see the flame in front of the bronze tiger?

The wick has blackened and at the base of the flame is a note of steely blue. Reflections shine red-gold.

Yesterday I walked again in the green space.

This has been thought for you.

Measures of Expatriation — II

The Prolongation of the Spine and the Stretched Neck Approximate the French Philosopher Only to His Own, and Airy, Beast

after Georges Bataille, 'La Bouche'

The mouth is planetary, circled by systematic tides. The molten core, the tongue-root; the microbial cities; the sirocco and austerities of breath.

★

The mouth is geographical to the extent that the body is terrain. The tiny life of flaking skin and self-mating thighs may exist and teem without language; the python inhabiting the buccal cavity may remain uninterpretable, too big to be perceived, by the atheistic dermal crowd.

★

The mouth is engineered by gender. In grief and anger, my sister's mouth will twist into a trap, it will not drop to let out the paroxysmal bellow which would be permitted her in childbirth; however and alas, her mouth seals itself, even her lips turn in as her eyes widen and the sinews in her neck become unmusically, why not furiously, strung.

★

The mouth is an anemone. See, in the dark wood it flowered and, sensing something, your hair raised up; but the social occasion smoked over your possible paths into the dark wood that flowered with promise and that tussored over the sleeping area of snakes.

★

The mouth is half of a knot. With my lips I tie you; our bodies are boat and floating jetty, our cinched animality no doubt locatable by the anxious Frenchman, who is rendered anxious because we have unnerved the chapterhouse of his skull and outside his studious window, oh so suddenly, cry after cry unnerves the night, as we prolong the ground as sea beneath his feet, as we slip (mouths knotted) out from the erotic vessels of ourselves, careless of the power to hurt or to do none.

INSIDE THE GATEWAY: 1970S RED CLOGS WITH SIDE BUCKLE

The forever shoe, which points homewards, belongs to my mother. When our house was being built, she stepped onto the driveway while the tarmac was still wet, still setting. Ever since that step, the driveway, which slants upwards, bears an imprint of her 1971 footwear. Her footprint says, *Climb! Come with me.* Whoever steps into that impression becomes, for a moment, the leggy wearer of a fire-red clog with a piratical silver buckle on the side.

OUTSIDE THE TEMPLE: GOLD AND SILVER SANDALS

The sandals which will make a female of me belong to many women. The front of the temple entrance hides itself behind shoe-racks. Visitors enter barefooted, leaving behind the dung, dried frogs, spilled petrol and ketchup traces of the streets. Hundreds of pairs of gold and silver sandals wait here for the women who will re-emerge from the vigil with the taste of basil leaf and sugar in their deep-breathing mouths and carpet fibres between their toes. The sandals, gold and silver, seem all alike. How can the women tell them apart? They do tell them apart. It is as if each pair sings an intimate mantra to its owner, audible only to her. One day I too shall return to expectant slippers that stack up like the moon and the stars outside a marble building; one day I shall not have to wear child's shoes.

SUNDAY BEFORE SCHOOL: WHITE SNEAKERS

Seven years of these shoes are a chemical memory. The Convent ruled that pupils' shoes must be white: absolutely white. Who can imagine a 1980s shoe that was absolutely white, without any logo, with no swoosh, not a single slogan? Sunday evenings, before the school week, I crouched down on the pink bathroom tiles and painted my shoes into the absolute of whiteness; like the Alice in Wonderland gardeners repainting roses. This task was performed with a toothbrush and with special paste that annihilated so many design features. Purity was attained by the application of a whitener that stank of scientific polysyllables. Convent-girl identity. Tabula rasa. Toxicity and intoxication: with good intentions, getting high on paste.

When I met my ex, I was already committed to heels: black ankle boots with four-inch stacks for walking through snow; French cream curved suède stilettos for scaling fire-escape ladders on to rooftops to admire the winter sky; even after I left him, scarlet satin bedroom-only spiky mules to amuse myself. Early on, my ex said that the way women walk in heels looks ugly. And my nails made unnatural social appearances: emerald lacquer; cobalt; incarnadine. Sign of a bad marriage: I began to wear flats. The penitential mermaid shoes, worn once and once only, were a Gabor creation: distressed silver ballet slippers with netted and criss-cross side details which would make the material seem to swish with the changes of light on feet that go walking. Cool as moonlight on a tourist coastline. But the inner stitching hooked the softness of my skin, which has always been too soft; but I could not turn back, for we had tickets to an evening of Mozart; but the paper tissues that I stuffed into my shoes failed to act as a protective lining. Paper tissue snow-flecks teardropped with crimson blood created a trail behind me as I ascended the many tiers of the wedding-cake concert hall.

BAREFOOT: PEARL PINK POLISH

Sitting next to someone can make my feet curl: shy, self-destructive and oyster-like, they want to shuck their cases, to present themselves, little undersea pinks; their skin still is too soft, their toes still too long, their ankles still too slender, for a modern fit. But he is not modern; he sits like stone, and my bare feet are cool, they will not have to bleed.

'I Love You'
for Geraldine Monk

'I love you,' he wouldn't say: it was against his philosophy; I-love-you didn't mean what it meant, plus the verray construction of the phrase caused bad-old-concrete-lawman-vandal-verbal-mildew-upon-the-grape-harvest-and-war-for-rare-minerals-required-to-manufacture-commu-nications-devices damage; saying I-love-you damaged love, subject and object; plus he could prove this in two dense and delphic languages suitable for philosophy, opera, cursing, and racking the nerves of arti-ficial intelligence machines that perhaps could love but would be hard-wired giammai to dare say so. So what moved him to not-say I-love-you? What wake-up-and-spoil-the-coffee ashtray-licking djinn? I have to start to agree. The verbness of it impropriety (eyes glob up the syringe when you're giving blood: semisolid spiralling); perhaps too active... I-love-you, I sand you, I drill you, I honey and set you for wasps, crimson you like a stolen toga, add value applying dye, fight owner-ship, I cite you to justify skilled outrage, put your name as guarantor on an astronomical mortgage, I admit desertification comes as a relief, from I to O, O my oasis, O my mirage. Maybe the verb is a tending-to-wards? A tightrope? A tropism? A station? But that's meeting him on his own ground; plus I can't disprove entire languages; plus those three little words aren't meant as saying. An icy drink in stormlight. A looked-at leaf left to transpire its own way until... And sans I-love-you the centuried moon rose above dinnermint stone; many men contin-ued talking; a woman lifted her sarsenet skirt, peed on green lilies and, utterly gracious, walked through the archway to join the mixed group delighting in – word! believe it! – fresh air.

Chloe on the Jubilee

for Shivanee Ramlochan

The staring heterosexuals disembark,
having stared, openly, having picked the direction
for their stares: a few cubic inches,
mostly compacted of woman; staring
like a newish smoking, asphyxiation by kilometres;
the disembarking heterosexuals pit
picador arms against the heads of females,
high-end climate-change cologne;
they have vetivered and tidalled out.
Two women, seated, remain
like money, like any underground objects,
like a philosophy of inexistence, like earliness, unperceived.
Soya latte meets box handbag
meets lack of a glossy magazine
meets lightweight summer brastrap,
countenance facing another, scarlet and opposite.

I need to delete the shortcut that is Timothy. He sold me the one and only futureproofed summer of my experience. Standing ankle-deep in wild garlic in a Sussex lane he spoke of roses, and I almost bought it; I almost bought it right then and there when a 4X4 careened down the middle of the national speed limit lane sprung with Tudor-looking hedgerows almost spiky enough to stick a row of heads on, and in a whiff of gasoline one of those very common rabbits paid the price of someone else's rich misuse of private transport and screamed time no longer.

I need to delete the shortcut that is Timothy. It was down the river that he sold me that summer. Wearing the feminist Germaine Cellier's *Bandit* perfume, which she formulated after sniffing the knickers straight off the models on a post-World War II runway... I actually bought it; I actually bought it, a scent that accelerates from a whiff of gasoline only to end in the cabinet, medicinal dead wood branching out into fatherly hangers.

I need to delete the shortcut that is Timothy but first I must delete Linda, because he added her, but if I delete Linda, I need to delete Susan, because they were on a jobshare and they were never more than workfriends, who should not have had any shortcuts anyway.

I didn't rightclick on Timothy. I leftclicked on Timothy. I'm opening Timothy. I remember the summer that was Timothy, but I do not recall what's inside Timothy. How many keystrokes have been wasted on Timothy...

Timothy contains seven folders: Wrath, Greed, Pride, Sloth, Lust, Envy and Gluttony. These names do not look right. It was a night to remember when I went into Timothy and renamed everything within Timothy. I do not recall that night. I do not wish to delve too deeply into the sevenfold contents of Timothy.

Timothy was a project manager and he made projections. Perhaps the sins correspond to the phases of our project; our futureproofed summer. Wrath is Thinking, Greed is Planning, Pride is Doing, Sloth is Monitoring, Lust is the Exit Phase leading to or perhaps including the Feedback of Envy, while there's no place in the scheme for Gluttony, which clearly means this guess is wrong. I might as well call the notes of a musical scale or name the colours of the rainbow as continue with this childish game. I'm hovering over and selecting the entirety of Timothy, about to finish him off.

Timothy had set the background of my laptop to roses, which used too much memory, making everything freeze, and he introduced a Trojan horse by unprotected browsing. There are babies in foreign lands named after Timothy by mothers he never met; many project workers relied remotely on Timothy.

Now it's all blue again and it's coming back to me. It's coming back to me since I'm deleting the shortcut that is Timothy.

What was most difficult was proving that it was suicide, though the irregular little room with vodka windows and cranberry shantung curtains in the hotel near to the railway station seemed made only for that or the other thing; but I had no interest in finishing off the real Timothy, who taught me that income and happiness are not linked, so whether I am worse off or better off since the death of the real Timothy makes no difference, especially since we are in crisis and also at war, and for such a long time I hung on to the shortcut that was Timothy. The real Timothy was philosophical; when it turned out that neither Susan nor Linda could spell, he said: at least we know where they were educated and that they'll have no choice but to listen to us when they make their choices; then he struck a deal under the table with the futureproofer from the rival company, a deal which seemed as if it could turn out to my advantage, though instead as you see I'm living in this different place now, with people like you.

And if the real Timothy were here he'd pluck out the heart of our mystery, reminding me that a positive correlation does not necessarily indicate a cause.

Though it's a pretty rotten coincidence that all my other icons vanished almost as soon as I'd deleted the shortcut that is Timothy; and the blue screen is bluer than you'd have thought.

María Lloró / Blue Sky Tears
for Maria Jastrzebska

Ministry of Tourism
edict:
henceforward, islanders, utilize
naturally strippable skies –
way to have
succeeded
since our bluedock
coats are shredded;
pitchy patchy citizenry
sailors,
rum 'uns, several-headed,
ordered to repair
indoors, permitted only
strictly
necessary sky-strips, un-
satisfying radical geo-
metría – ay, María,
azul
celestial's glued beneath
pinked nails, jiffed
away multiplicatory trapezium
smiles,
leaving this oval
blank of face –
qué hacer, flat-out
cielo
emplasters our changing-room;
if window glazing
wipes out outsideness –

Me
extraña tu ausencia,
absent carnivaller, auditor;
specks of dust
general
all over island,
(dóndequiera, mi general)
who's to rationalize
(merced)
our clean-up job?

Estamos listos. Bring

the Google car.
Presentable.
We're readied by
being gone again.

Inhuman Triumphs
for Nicholas Laughlin

(I) THE POET TRANSFORMED INTO A BOX HEDGE

it was a small snail
on a rainy day
it was a small snail
a petal vertex
it was a small snail
nestled ascendant
the heart of a rose
an apricot rose
and for a small snail
on a rainy day
the sea was beating
about my heart; O
love, beating about
my green heart of hearts

(II) THE POET TRANSFORMED INTO A DOUBLE VODKA

Accuse me, before I start,
of seeking forms to shatter –
at the icy least, to overspill –
you, meantime, pouring out me
on the rocks. MAN DRINKS MERMAID
MISTAKING HER FOR LIQUOR!
Seizing my mirror, make up
wars for islands that aren't cold;
you grin; I chill; water wins my heart,
an alien drop in my interior
and into whom I'm melting,
a cubic volume of undrunk spirit; O
love, wrapt in glass wrapt in a set of bony fingers...
Air, how does it transpire that we are from each other?

(III) THE POET TRANSFORMED INTO A HEAT HAZE

& it was not a hot country; but occasionally
hot, though not by decree nor description; even a day
like this, where it rained fiercely on sheets of sun, jubilant
about heat, but denying hotness; not a hot country.
& it drove the insects in droves, it drove drivers off roads,

drove drivers into whatever grows on the sides of roads
& roads became what happened to be passing by, because
I melted them; & beggars died too shy to beg for drinks
because it's stupid to feel the heat, admit to feeling
the heat & to not liking it & not to liking it
but to feeling everything twice as thick, feeling at all;
the stream sucked it up, milled on wordless; the trees rebelled, O
love, voted with their roots, forgetting how to vote, vowing
their all to – as a leaf double, shape, shade, light – a stitch-up –

(IV) THE POET TRANSFORMED INTO A PIECE OF PAINTED FABRIC

That night laid hands on my back,
ironing out a castle,
finding no body, is true;
that night's pursuit turned up
a green sleeve flat as a wall,
that's true as well; sky & I
locked eyes; who called curtains first
no journalism could tell. Shall this
poem turn to the wrong side?
A fine seam of gold stripes me;
righteous buyers mutter, *mined*;
mine, I said to night. And O
love, night kept going round in circles,
trailing a moonless shower, lyrid threads.

(V) THE POET TRANSFORMED INTO SPACE

****
~~L'amor che move il sole e l'altre stelle~~
~~L'amor che move il sole e l'altre stelle~~
~~L'amor che move il sole e l'altre stelle~~
~~L'amor che move il sole e l'altre stelle~~
~~L'amor che move il sole e l'altre stelle~~
~~L'amor che move il sole e l'altre stelle~~
****
****
~~sphere gas gravity heat radiation collapse~~
~~luminosity colour temperature location~~
****
*************************************** * O
love,   *

Measures of Expatriation — III

Neomarica Sky Jet
for Helena Taylor

GIVE ME YOUR REASONS

that I may have tokens
by which to remember you
no please no more keeping in touch
you have already taken so much
of myself from myself, reinvested
in paragraphs to your prosaic advancement –
keynote speaker hired to dust off archival blues –
give me your reasons

THESE WORDS, THOSE MOST CRYING THINGS

a poem
possible, consisting
not of those things
he meant to write about –
a poem: merely
word reminders
after some tumult
that embarrassed him
into writerpoise –
small change,
high voltage,
burning his own
adjustable light.
and these words, those most crying things –
sunk for now
in his private code,
like his 'moonrise' stands in
for black black tree
since felled,
street lamp
once upon a time
unrepaired,
across the road
alsatianed and unplayed-with
shotgun neighbours

in three pinkish storeys
(all this
his 'moonrise'),
and night
adamant leveller
pushing blues
on a land
already halfhearted
about difference
(this too coded
in his 'moonrise')
from big-word-
originary, and rising, sea

OUR OFFICES

This poem isn't his. So let us leave him,
nary a flicker in his groin: only
when those no-longer-his-kind hoist defeat
in their homeward eyes; televised killer
whales fountainpen ice floes;
violin-case nails,
lower-salary-scaled, female, tip off
from the everest of reception orchids
insects camped in uncompliant dormancy:
only then a flicker in his groin. So
let us leave him. This poem was not his.
It is the window's. The precipitant window's.
The window, who believes in this poem
it is the only thing personified;
grieving after wholeness, split in glass sheets,
steel-sheathed, lethal to the weather. New York
rains New York: different, technological,
skyscrapery grey rain; heart-of-a-pearl
chorusing out of the gutters... One drop!
The window's gripped by hopeless passion. That
one drop! that isn't personified! So,
this poem is the window's. (You're a star.)

SHE SAYS

Does it suit me? holding up
red cloth tacked in some fashion –

hoping that colour flicks on
redemption like a farm-shop
bauble, gleeful fruit of joy
seeded throughout colder days –
and she speaks
full of glorious veins,
anxious over scarlet rayon.
          Who
could have an objection; have
her as an object? She is
no thing; she is everything.
          Who says:
Poem, like a clasping knife
shut in safe relationship,
guard what you're made to cut out?

NEOMARICA SKY JET

Why, one of us, sitting
in a raw-hemmed purple garment's
softer flag, where the sand's flare
maximal against jade water
demarcates the old dance-massacre,
wished the other also sitting
at a marred dance-step's distance,
not as you and I sit
now and there
at unadaptive distance,
making as if perfectly aligned
          And she has lifted or lowered her arms
          she-who-rips-open-intention
          for this is in time without warfare
          time in between
          her scattering-of-sinews dance
Sand queers itself as light retreats
sea blue at last and last
neomarica sky jet
one and/or both of us sitting
the wish the distance
less and also perfectly aligned

Cities in Step
for the Weyward Sisters

talk about sleeping
you dream in black and white
i dream in fauve and phosphor

cities where people are held for interrogation
cities where taxidrivers and policemen
systematize their criminality
cities where the friends i can depend on
meet for the first time outside and by chance
mispronouncing hello
cities where the script is not quite Roman
crying out is currency
and so are sweets

i dream cities overwhelmingly
not people
you dream of flowers, dreaming you are
a girl

clothes shopping
you say what colour suits me
you see what colour suits me
is i-see-no-one-enter colour
is try-the-shop-three-miles-away colour
is would-your-friend-like-to-sign-up-for-the-newsletter-and-the-
                                        prize-draw colour
is you-probably-aren't-looking-for-anything-expensive colour
is oh-sorry-i-thought-you-were-together colour
you
aren't you with him
his hair disinterred from a scalp hung in basements
his skin pocked and bubbling spread under soil
his shoulders reaching down to smoosh his elbows
his hands growing in your direction
how else do we know you are here?
didn't you come with him
into our sunglasses shop
our expensive sunglasses shop
isn't he the one wanting
polarized designer lenses
why are you behaving
as if you are not with him?

he came in behind you; aren't you
together?

step from there

absolutely no change
and a good face on it
absolutely no change
let's go for a picnic
absolutely no change
we have the same basked
absolutely no change
how was your day? Did
you do, have, get, like, buy,
eat, drink, make up, make out
like you don't
dream cities
overwhelmingly?

we have spread a cloth on the ground
share another cloth over our knees
pass a flask without commenting
fireflies, their matchbox likeness,
pulled out like a thought of thinking
or of polar exploration,
Scott of the Antarctic, the taste
of chocolate dismissing him, death
seeming more New World, more Aztec
something my company will not
translate

talk about sleeping
being happy
i dream giraffes mostly
having put one together
from sand under seawater
dappled by sunlight
at paddling depth
or having seen it rise up
amiable
companionable
with a friendliness seldom measured by scientists
a long-lashed
essentially solitudinous yet
occasionally-leaning giraffe

truly i wanted
to build bridges
reinforced with bamboo
and a castle
using the classic
spade and bucket
where living shells
cut or sink
tiny silent circles
hissing with air
and what happened
the colour of
black happened, rainbow
which is black
happened, changed texture
happened, propulsive odour
happened to invade
hopes of building
we were playing
on the beach
and found oil
and looking at
the map's edge
we'd often drawn
in schoolroom pencil
where, grown-up, we'd
come to play
suddenly the air
filled with technologized
wings, the sand
spurted into wells,
though that moment
it was still
we were alone
nor been told
to frack off

step from there
now dream of flowers, dream we are
both girls, not people
girls overwhelming cities
crying out
sweetening
sleep

'I Wish to Be Speaking to You until Death'

for Jeremy Hardingham

The types of dead hedges
they plant here; choose
to plant what will rustle,
ornamental,
unreassuring, cling
death-in-life, rust-orange
leaves – we must walk
their lengths of deadness,
marred plantings.

The curse of barrenness
is unmodern;
so also a body
able to bear
its perambulations
only as weight,
touch being the kick
into killing,
unworded, internal.
This kind of body
has no smashed leg,
mobility device,
gold loping guide;
has no current token
to be exchanged
for consideration.
No self-publication.
Only a smile
to be relied upon.

The second head,
which is its real one, floats
like a balloon
reporting on the town:
frightful riots
in Body; Perspex shields
advancing, so
Body can be quelled, hosed,
re-presented
clothed, though contact
zones of cloth
and corpse need

scorched-earth treatment;
no love, no time.

No, love.

No time.

You will be angry
I am direct:
even that night when
you made incursions upon
some body, all you did
was floor my clothes;
next day I picked up, sure
sore somehow, in
the chronic time delay
where your being
at all – let alone
your
anger – becomes
a thing I ought to have
remembered, ought
to have been told, out of
politeness; oh,
to whom? Perhaps the lamp
resembles my head,
the door handle
your
penis;
I might locate
a radius
in a vase of feathers
or an ulna
pacifying a pelvis
in pleated blinds.

Put them all in my skin,
if you can; hear
the roof-ripping wind sigh
through left-over
plum blossom – there it is,
before you ask *put where,
put them back where?*

My skin the wind, it's gone
kiting; sew how
it is unfit

Measures of Expatriation — IV

for Judy Raymond

Terribly terribly sorry (not) it's hard relating
to this one: you know, the dead wench in another country,
gifted but an attention-seeker? Your camera strikes
from afar. Like snakes licking out K.'s ears, men of power
seem caught up with her. More Twitter than other girls round her.
Your camera strikes. K.'s screwing up her eyes in a boat –
speaking for the sisterhood, but from that kind of family?
Why listen? She's privilege. Complication. Must be spoilt.
K.'s voice flares victim to her high-explosive hair; her thoughts
dismissable; cuntly, if you're a man; peripheral.

Take sixty seconds to re-read each of the lines above.
That took ten minutes: half as long as my death by stoning.

> Athena, grey-eyed, justicer,
> they've brought me back
> as if each stone
> broken for their roads
> and the rare earths
> mined for their devices
> vocalized my far-flung blood,
> but I have questions
> for you, law-giver, spoiler;
> also, plans to find
> which women you move
> in these greater days
> of privilege and complication.
> Holding on to you
> was the safe zone
> but the hero entered
> held and raped me
> in your precincts, justicer.

Why'd you let him do it? Why did you wait to strike him down?
Was it, in a way I do not understand, due process?

Does the burden of proof still fall on me, in modern courts?
As people encouraged by helpful foreigners to cross
a minefield may smile, stretchered, blinded or their legs blown off,
so each of my memories, a living and willing witness,
gets up to walk to you, to tell my story, but doesn't
make it. His camera strikes from afar. If you want it
to add up, why give me the gift of prophecy? I split,
spill truth like marrow from bones, gleaming on stone-strewn ground.

The Book of Dreams / Livre de Cauchemars

for JanaLee Cherneski

I

The women were helpful. The smart cut of their suiting would be elegance in England. In this country it meant that they did not work for themselves. They would be slashed and draped if they were independent. Their suiting bespoke an important, insecure job.

The helpful women were to one side of me wherever we went: the semi-open corridors along the side of concrete quadrangles; the raw rooms with class-length chipboard trestle tables; the half-built, much-used places still to be crossed, topsoil red-orange from sand mixed into sea-reclaimed, or de-agriculturalized, earth.

Something was wanted. I trusted there were good intentions.

Through grilled walls the semi-pleased students were to be seen: standing; sitting; a bewilderment of orderliness and familial pride.

Something was wanted. I would be agreeable.

We were sitting down, with a few more of the women. How good some of what they said they did was!

What did they stand for? I did not want to agree to something.

A ringbound notebook was given to me. A notebook as large as a music book was given to me. A large notebook with a laminated cover was given to me. A shiny green notebook was given to me, recalling the carapace of an insect seldom seen these days.

Inside were rough photocopies, cut-and-paste jobs, blurry, some photocopied from typescripts bad in the original. Verse extracts featured, with space beside and in between the stanzas.

Was that extract Tennyson? Here I could not recognize Tennyson. Were his lines so complex and so long, or had they undergone development in the process of copying?

The women's looks were anxious. The women's mouths scraped an expression. The women's focus was as neat as thimbles.

I would live in the barracks. I would update the verse. I would make it relevant. I would employ dialects. Then I would use the verse as a basis of teaching. There were lambsfuls of students to be taught.

II

The land was flat and round. A river, as if it would have been blue anyway, reflected the sky. It was hard to discern it as river. It ran in loops. There was no way of crossing directly to where we were going. Nor was the destination in view. The distance was amethyst mist. People zigzagged for miles ahead. This had the appearance of leisure.

The people might be struggling across the tussocked mud of the vast, but they did not have to crowd.

The national power grid had gone out. It was said that water reserves would be hit next. That was why we had been put on the move. The town across from us had a considerable water reservoir.

Walking towards it, as yet we could see nothing. People did not know about the water. They were supposed to know about the electricity. Those of us who knew about both should help to keep people moving, without saying. There was no alarm.

Nice ladies expected to go home soon. They sauntered like daytime, greying hair deliberate in its yellowing, orange linen skirts ethically traded, blue flowered dresses having cost a pound and a crown. They brandished folk chic baskets, having taken few things. They chatted through strong teeth.

I would not normally have been on a walk with such nice ladies. They would go to church where they lived. They would book into the restaurants where I lived. They had children, with related activities out of town, requiring the car. Now they were most concerned that school might be disrupted. Assessment tests had been scheduled. Their children must not lose pace.

Losing pace, place, face, without children, having nothing to join, I walked without saying: aspirins, spectacles, flour, there will be none of these things. The factories, and the mills of God, alike will stop grinding.

None of these things entered their vision.

Fine, lagging, sauntering.

I tried to maintain a sense of direction.

In the distance was water. At our backs, the town, on which darkness had fallen. Day persisted, eggshell and semiprecious. I could not see with whom, but we had to keep up.

III

Night in another place. Again the having to keep walking. I know this road. It runs south to the next town, which over a thousand years ago was the greater, and accessed by river. I stick to the western side of this road. It is a broken way, not meant for pedestrians. The pavements give way to grass verges that dip into the straggle of nothing. They are in the dark but in daylight diffuse anyhow, returning to hedgerow and hostility at the least opportunity: sports grounds, a parking lot, lower middle-class terraced housing latterly subdivided if not subsidized for the less poor, fish and chips, a shop of middle-price reclaimed pine, and the stretches of nothing.

It was on this road in one of the great floods of the early twenty-first century that the young mother saw the man wading throw up his

arms with a strange jerk and fall: electrocuted, as she learned later.
But she had to keep wading. He was closer to town than I.
Still the having to keep walking.

I think a house owned by my parents may have been somewhere
further to the west and south, almost in the woods, the occasional
deer startling the infrequent transport. Black and damp around the
edges as any wood, on the way that could be the way there, tonight.
The cars few, the street lights more and more spaced out, the road
south the road to nothing.

I begin to decide to turn, feeling the widening and flattening under-
foot that meant imminent crossroads. Two friends almost bump
into me. Who are they? The one I know better was a curled darling,
palefaced like a dollmaker's temps perdu. The other I know less.
Both so pleased to see me! Their faces bob, charge, glimmering up,
losing themselves and returning: let's go for a drink! Night is ocean
in a barrel.

Yet we keep walking down the dark road. The places that sell drink
are at our backs, some distance in the other direction, except for
one, unpleasant at the best of times, to the left across the road that
widens to a savagery of raggedness. We stop.

On our side of the crossroads, from the right, a girl in a short mossy
green velvet dress. She hangs back slightly from the pool of street-
light. She must have made her way from the place that was almost
woods, where (I think) is a house once owned by my parents. Her
smile announces her as another friend. Hadn't we met twice or so?
She can join us for a drink! Perhaps it is an effect of the hour, of the
light. Perhaps it is too much effort to have legs. But hers taper away
to a wisp of shadow like the tail of a fish glimpsed submerged.
Look! she laughs. The grass lifts like a lid. It's fun! In a blink she
is tucked in to the curling-space. The lid of grass does not have to
be closed or re-opened. In a blink she is out through the hinge of
it. She stands on the pavement where she was before. Try it! She
encourages me more than the others. I can see that anyone would
get in. I doubt that I can manage her trick of getting out. I let myself
into the space. The lid of grass ripples and shrugs. It is shutting
over me, as it did not shut over her. I push the human way, with
hands. You see, I couldn't do it like you.

She sulks, seeming to recede on the spot towards the woods, with
no more legs than before.

IV

The facelessness. The friendliness. These professionals. Are they
dressed for indoors or outdoors? The colours of their fabrics are
determined on irresolution: beige into khaki, grey into grey, via

amethyst, heather, forest, mist, taupe, steel, sea blue, seal pelt. This
is the expensive version of washable. They are dressed to be iron-
proof, rollsafe, rucksackworthy; casual, smart. I cannot tell.
We left town where town had given up on being town. The roads
led out big and broad like hope in a school-syllabus anthem. Their
surfaces maintained an impressive evenness while what was around
them changed. Arcades and parking lots thinned out. Here and
there was an ornamental shrub specially planted next to a specially
placed single bench next to the round base of an upturned litter bin
recumbent on the mown razor grass where nobody sat with sand-
wiches. Cars ran past. There were no vendors walking between the
traffic and no stalls along the road. Nobody would have stopped.
With no sense of having left the car or whose car had driven me I
have been walking for a long time. Brown shoes, not mine, stand up
to being scuffed as they keep going. The dust I kick up is cousin to
orange pine ice cream. Tree roots smell fresh, like the gutters at an
open-air butcher's. That means snakes.
The quiet surge of grey and brown is my friends behind me, moving
like sea in a documentary viewed with the sound off.
The leaves, green and yellow, invite a holiday mood. Herded into
dappled shade, I go willingly.
The sound begins, in the form of questions.
– What about V. S. Naipaul? – I had twenty-three first cousins, until
one (not him) died. And he is not even one of those. – Is he your uncle?
– My father's first cousin. I don't know how many first cousins my
father had. He is dead too. – You have read V. S. Naipaul. What about
V. S. Naipaul in the fifties and sixties? Was he in England then? – I was
born in Trinidad, in 1973. – What about possible Soviet connexions
for V. S. Naipaul? – That is absurd, I thought people said he wanted
to be British. – Many Caribbean writers had Soviet connexions in the
fifties and sixties; Andrew Salkey wrote *Havana Journal*. Or did they? –
I was born in Trinidad, in 1973. – What about possible radical femi-
nist and pro-abortion connexions for V. S. Naipaul? – That is absurd,
I thought people suspected him of misogyny. – What about the prac-
tice of abortion in the Hindu community using traditional methods
of massage or the insertion of bamboo sticks? Abortion is in most
cases illegal in Trinidad. Is there no coded reference to that in any of
Naipaul's writings? – I have not read all of Naipaul's writings. I very
much doubt it. – What about possible animal rights connexions for
V. S. Naipaul? Doesn't he promote vegetarianism? – But almost no-
body in that family is a true vegetarian, myself included. I remember
seeing my grandfather splitting a stewed fish skull and picking out
the white brains with a fishbone, to eat them. I was only little. He let
me have some brains and I enjoyed them.– How did V. S. Naipaul get
his writing promoted? – I don't know anything about getting writing
promoted. I thought V. S. Naipaul did his best to record his precise

vision of things. – Is V. S. Naipaul a Trinidadian writer, a British writer, or an Indian writer? – Wasn't V. S. Naipaul born British anyway? People in Trinidad were all British before Independence. Not everybody automatically changed. – What about possible – They would not let it go. We were well into the woods.

V

It was not a holiday but we were going to this house by the beach. Just my mother, and a friend who had escaped from her family for half a day. There were no tourist facilities and the house did not belong to a village. It had a roof but no ceiling. The main room, hall-like, peaked at around twenty feet. The trestle table inside was cheap wood but covered with a white cloth. The metal folding chairs were stackable and chipped, oxblood paint under the gun-grey paint. A few were set around the table. The house belonged to a man who was tall. His curly hair, full of sea salt, almost made dreads. I did not like the way that my mother and my friend both knew him and smiled at him. I had not expected him or even the presence of his house in this place. Now it was clear that if all went well perhaps I would marry him.

The dirt where anything could grow ran out abruptly. The rough tussocks of lawn became skimpier and interspersed with bone-white sand. A graceful curve of coconut trees huddled up to the house as if marking a garden boundary. I had never seen coconut trees planted this way before. Their normality was the wind's wild punctuation. Planned planting belonged to inshore mansions, tulip trees and (if there was room) cassia.

Still he was smiling at me and in his cutoff trousers he half-danced his way into the very turquoise sea. Three-foot waves chopped up the tideline. He turned around with his back to the horizon. The curls waved. His eyes were bright.

I like the sea. I started walking into it.

He laughed and started walking backwards. Then the sea chopped at me and laid rope after rope around my calves and ankles. I staggered on the spot.

He laughed and continued walking backwards. I felt drawn towards where the sun sinks.

Anyone who has been knocked down by a wave in such clear Atlantic water and kept their eyes open (accustomed from young to the salt) will have seen the epitome of nothing. The force of the wave's crash raises a sandstorm beneath the sea. As the wave retreats, the undertow pulling the felled bather with it, clouds of sand silently roar in changing formations. The desert sandstorm advances as the wave retreats. The open-eyed bather feels all her limbs being dragged

under, some of the water chill with the chill of deep sea, while her
eyes are confounded by the utter and absolute darkness beneath the
stirring sand. It is a lightlessness like no other.

He stood too tall and too far immersed in the sea, looking like
brightness. It would be death to join him. Did the women expect it?

With the greatest effort I began to turn and found them looking
appalled. They called my name. I dragged myself upright to shore.
Whether or not he in the sea had vanished I do not know; his satis-
faction was at my back and his house was still in front of me. I felt
he was many.

My mother and my friend welcomed me as if there had been no
changes.

I asked to leave the seaside and start finding our way home.

VI

Someone had developed the bay since our last visit. The drive north
was the same as for the more famous bathing-place; only a little
further. We parked and began the uncertain walk (what should the
feet expect? blown sand over paved path, or deep sand? mud or
quicksand? broken bottle or quartz?), to arrive at the tight little curve.

The lines in the sea threw up walls of light, drawing an imaginary
stadium around the bay – an under-resourced stadium whose build-
ing contractor had run off with the cash: the walls of light, lined like
sea, were like corrugated metal, grey and splashed with rust or the
red of rained-on national slogans.

It wasn't a question of us arriving late: the grey and rust, scrub and
dust, in a place indubitably holiday destination-ish for the people
who lived on the island even more than for the thin-on-the-ground
tourists. Up till the previous bend in the road, the day had retained
its colour.

The match had not started.

We walked down the steep slope to what was not defined enough
to be a beach – more the area belonging to the sea. The ground
was damp-packed, indicating that sometimes but not always it was
below water. We turned left, or south-west, and up a smaller slope.

The pleasant, ramshackle new hotel, two and a half storeys high,
overlooking the bay, had an old-fashioned gallery running the
length of each floor. Perhaps not belonging to the hotel, there was a
not-imaginary slice of stadium, or rather seats in tiered stands and
something like a barbecue area, covering the western part of the
angle of the small bay. That was new. It looked worn.

The match was starting. We sat on metal folding chairs in the first
floor gallery, to watch the boys play football in the sea.

'Eh-eh! But what are you doing here!' It was the drum majorette from the Form II March Past parade – how many years ago? Grown up now, pretty in red, with a frosty can of something in her hand. Retired headmistresses. Half-remembered prefects. Everybody's aunt in a flowered hat and coral lipstick, the weight of a picnic cooler testing the strength of her talcum-thick wrist. Somebody's father (but hadn't he died?) trying harder to be friendly since he had betrayed his wife. The boys from the College of the Immaculate Conception, out of uniform and in red or white cotton T-shirts that burned and cowled over the forbidden meagreness that, shyly and muskily, was – not their bodies –was also–them. Other boys from their college were in the sea, all at sea, playing football in the sea.

We were gathered there together to watch the match.

How were they managing it? Their knees were lifting above the waves. Despite the absence of goalposts, and the shifting depth of water, the boys seemed to know where to go. They were playing side-on to the waves; side-on to us. The waves came in faster, following one another like one ridged iguana moving from branch to branch. The boys were thin and whippy like coconut trees, heads ferocious clusters of concentration.

'The match going well!'

But a dark cloud was blowing up, between the open sea and the edge of mountain. And the boys would not stop playing. And the wind was blowing up too, chill and bitter and salt, what the Atlantic brings to the tropics and is not 'tropical'. The drops of rain then, heavy like one cent coins, hitting us like spiteful alms. And the boys seemed unable to stop playing. And they were kicking the ball up somehow from under greater and greater depth of water, and we remarked their sportsmanship from their elbows, the tops of their torsos, the struggling coconut-heads above the waves, in between the waves. They were in deeper. The sea was nearer. Nearer to us. We were not enjoying watching the boys playing football in the sea.

They were playing the match of their lives.

Under the rimlet of every wave gasping further up on to the damp-packed ground, the sea brought more darkness.

Then the approximate stadium of the bay began, most impressively, to acquire a fourth wall.

The Atlantic was going to join the match, and come in to the hotel afterwards.

Louise Bourgeois: Insomnia Drawings
Fruitmarket Gallery, Edinburgh, 2013
for Rod Mengham

FELT PEN

'Tell me why she – '
She. Shush, shush, shush. She.
A heap of she, as if asleep but not asleep
she stirs, her bed of pins untucked;
transforms and tiptoes out,
a high-heeled bird
whose own actions plucked away
the concentrated bits,
the beak that makes the bird.
'Tell me why she – '
She. Shush, shush, shush. She.
She speaks in pens and is not heard.
A sheep. A peasant-bellied caryatid.
Anatomical cabaret. Each pore of the skin
has edges that kick out like legs
and not only the eyes twitch,
but also the unaccredited folds of flesh:
the submarine corners of the gums,
the urgent or abject pleating within hinges,
ankleflanks and wristchrysanthemums,
kneedeeps and elbowcunts.
Something of a relief then,
that the tongue of insomnia burns,
a wafer of metal,
an instrument with which to score
another sostenuto non senza piacere ma quasi senza fine
long night's journey into night.
'Tell me why she – '
'If it weren't 'Louise Bourgeois'
we wouldn't – '
'Tell me why she used a red felt pen.'
'Because a red felt pen is Freudian.'
'Because felt is fuzzy, and she's female.'
'Because red is menstrual.' 'Labial.' 'Dangerous.' 'Primal.'
'A come-on. A stop-short.
Lucky. Risky. Demonic. Popish.'
'Wetter than blue. Hotter than yellow.'
'Because a red felt pen is
a substitute for the phallus,

and also for an American flag stripe
signifying the absence of France.'
Because it was there.
'What?'
Because –
'Oh. If it wasn't Louise Bourgeois
who was using a red felt pen,
we wouldn't be – '
Because it was bloody well there,
and in a fix or in a fit, the artist
fiercely repurposes whatever is to hand.

DANS LE JARDIN DE MA MÈRE

this was not work meant for your sight
this was not the work of one night
a lipstick strike
a rose grows
eyelash
wet flash
mathematic
grows oblique
from the river
lift its peaks
but leave its flow
from each finger
knifes the heat
of what they know
years of marks
to make a rose
how to pull space
apart, extract
concentrique
essence of rose
this was not the work of one night
this was not work meant for your sight

friend sheep, if i stretched wide enough
i could give birth to a child like you:
a round-eyed barrier against normality,
a rare breed indeed, not a marie antoinette pet.
legendary plus que prehistoric.
a sheep like you at my knees
and pre-ruined trade routes at my feet,
and we would be in Sumeria.

dans la nuit it was lost, a closet heterosexual;
my children's successful sleep rendering me antimaternal
as if my body had not gaped, was a gap, was immaterial.
so I placed my hands between my legs, found fleece,
began to pull, till wonderstruck i ushered you
into my studio, away from the world, from the waking world.

peaceable and only slightly sinister
since languageless and eager in your bleating
about the silence brushing up against us from all sides,
my darling newborn ancient beast,
unboxed and not for sacrifice.

i count on you. take us away.
cross another and another stile.
nibble your way through the hedge of mist
springing from the Hudson,
through the thorns of light thrown up
by the Atlantic; voyage safely, amicable sheep,
into France; no questions asked.

i would flatten with you into tapestry,
my hair and yours washed by handfuls in the river,
vu que, in profound night and these circonstances,
it is déjà as if insomnia hangs us, already
hooked to a wall.

In this esquisse, the snake, if Freudian, is phallic, simple and part of
a complex in the quasi-scientific sense, rather than being the rustling
thing that sheds its skins and lives by seasons and for reasons not for
our making out.

> Insert a logical connector here; c'est ce qui
> manque dans ce texte.

This snake, however, seems to be related to the snake from the it-is-
not-a-children's-book written and illustrated by Saint-Ex, ace pilot and
seducer, Antoine de St-Exupéry.

> A logical connector is not necessary here; his territory was the

desert, and I speak

> in tongues of insomnia, metal wafers that burn.

In the book of St-Exupéry, the first serpent was a boa; more exactly,
boa fermé, a phrase which means neither a farmed boa nor a boa sau-
vage, but rather a closed boa that had swallowed an elephant and in its
suède distension was misapprehended by adult viewers who did not
discern a boa in replete speedhump profile, but a somewhat lop-sided,
well-worn hat.

> Here the logical connectors are supplied
> by the audience as if in a collective
> dream: a dream of waking, and of waking
> again, and waking with an effort, trying to force the
> buds of day-name and doorknob, but
> after all these wakings, waking only
> into sleep.

Accordingly, the snake Louise Bourgeois has placed to slide as snakes
do: as if reversing gravity, their remarkable unity of woven muscle
being the art that conceals art: this snake perches, as if sheepish, on
the slope of a mound not so difficult to ascend – this snake is over-
looked not by a little planet with its boy and rosebush, such as orbits
through the pictures in St-Ex's book – this snake finds itself observed
by a web-centric spider which has a jubilant air, as do most spiders, as
if let in on the secrets of time – this snake, if taken to be at best akin to
the boa escaped from the arid pages of St-Ex, appears to be climbing
partway over itself, over a boa fermé from which both boa and swal-
lowed elephant have been rubbed out, reduced to outline which, being
line, has perhaps direction, but no thickness.

> In conclusion, this snake is hors de soi,

> expelled by its own process.

Poor, menacing, insomniac snake, self-exiled from the warm rolling
hill of its digestion; a snake no longer contentedly, interiorly afloat.

I can draw like that, exactly like that! I mean, when I doodle.
I'm still surfacing. I had a thought...
And I know someone who can draw exactly like that!
) birds and bushes
My boss. She always doodles.
) scatter graphs and stick figures
I was doodling like that on a telephone pad when I was two!
) bees and daisies
Just like that.
) treble clefs and labyrinths
Yes, like that.
) spirals, stars and traps
I made and struck down lines, arrayed and
manœuvred shapes as if I'd been obsessed with
fractals all my life (I did read Tom Stoppard's
Arcadia when I was sixteen). There was something
I didn't share with Louise Bourgeois, however:
unlike poor young Louise, forced by circumstances into
working with her parents, who were tapestry restorers,
I was not a victim of child labour, did not have
to identify, mend or invent intricate patterns;
that must have been heavy, washing all those
big cloths in the river; heavy and unquestionably
very French.
Well, although I was lucky enough not to
lose my childhood or anything like that, there
was a creative interval: I went to a Montessori
school. You should have seen my play mat:
a sculpture park of red and blue plasticine!
Have you seen enough?
It punched a hole in me
when we moved house; a great quavering
black hole.
So I can relate to that.
Anyone can draw like that. It's like
saying tongue-twisters, or singing very high
for very long.
) je veux et j'exige
) du jasmin et des jonquils
) daft for daffodils
It comes out a bit different
if it's a coloratura like Kiri Te Kanawa
warbling in the shower –
) insist on lilies

Not a bit!
Would you have to think
at some level
about music –
Not a bit!
all the time –
It's a glug of notes, is all.
Something on my mind to say to you.
Lost the thread. Tip of my tongue,
burning metal wafer insomniac tongue.

'I GIVE EVERYTHING AWAY': A PARCEL CONTAINING THREE (3) SLEEPS
(CUSTOMS & RESALE VALUE NIL): UN CADEAU POUR MADAME

Dear Louise Bourgeois,

In helpless admiration, I place at the threshold
of your lidless doodles a parcel of unlikely sleeps, sleeps which I have
ascended like slopes and others that overcame me like waves; for as
the action of sleep on the body is obvious, so should the words be,
stunning like a mallet falling off the wall onto the head of a folktale
fool, all-assuming like a politician pressing the doorbell to a block of
flats where the time-decayed wiring has morphed into tufts within the
ears of the bricks; sleep, being the gentlest aggressor, assembles these
words and gangs up on you; sleep gangs up, for sleep presents as sev-
eral, a sundering and dissolution of already-unstuck selves, and one
sleep passes into another sleep; and in bringing you the confession
of unlikely sleeps, I wish for you, too late, wakefulness as a choice;
for insomnia is the violent partner of sleep, it is an abuse of time that
resembles chosen vigil as a condemnation resembles a destiny, as a
compulsion resembles artistic decision, as despair resembles espoir,
as an alternative resembles a joyful need; as tuning up resembles
music, as settling resembles true love.

The First Unlikely Sleep

Did not want to wake up in the hospital. No. Reorder words. In the
hospital. Did not want to wake up. Wanted not to wake up.

In the other life had been the eight-year-old lying across two chairs;
the bursting appendix; vomiting in the hallway under the peaky-roofed
building's nursing-home witch's hat; the political nurses in a free and
democratic election year summing up the parents by race, by class;
the unfinding of surgeons; the disavailability of anæsthetists. Almost

the last known to the child, before the chasm to be made in its flesh.
Months later, too well known, the expressive brimming, dollops of colour from the chasm, the side that would not squeeze shut.

General anæsthetic provoques numbness. General anæsthetic precludes dreams. Nonetheless dreams displaced anæsthesia. Nonetheless busyness displaced numbness. Busyness is proper to sleep and to dreaming. As rivers are the salient characteristic of a watercourse's redirection, both depth and surface, so the nearness of consciousness is a grand source of sleep and of dreaming. In a building with many levels, many people moved, whose murmured speech kept the child enthralled, awake within the dream within the melting anæsthetic, feeling no inclination towards a second waking.

I wish for you, too late, I wish sleep as a happy occupation.

The Second Unlikely Sleep

Madame, just as your clock, in having twelve hours, truly has twenty-four, and just as the unclosing eye, egged on by objects that would have preferred their secret nocturnal life to remain unobserved, undisturbed, just as that wakeful eye turns opaque like a steel ball bearing and refuses to take a view, drawing instead from that which is most inward – the telephone-wire spine, the peaks that the mind (after the fact of the sketch by the hand) might rationalize as life-and-soul-of-the-city pulses but that are even more inward, registering the nervous agony of enfleshed mathematics informing us of our kinship with patterns of music, copulation, rooftiles and rain – just so I wish to lay, alongside and between this metring-by-gallery of your insomnia, a little simplicity: the sleep I stole from a song in a hall where my ex stood enraptured by a swimsuited guitarist who plunged about in a state of girlish roaring; hear how fast, sound and simple this sleep when I climbed into immunity to external stimuli and, careless of what was being amplified all around me, careless even more of my ex's emotions, like a centipede curled inside a fur slipper, like your dead husband hogging the duvet, found a flat surface and slept.

I wish, too late, I wish to give you that rest.

The Third Unlikely Sleep

You took to using sheets of music paper, if at first because they were there, soon for their other and purposeful powers of signification.

My mother has great trouble practising staccato on the piano with her arthritic fingers. She tries out the meant-to-be-rapid-fire movement note by note. From these detached, successive efforts, a shape of music emerges. It is as if the idea of bread can be established from a loaf with the crumb pecked away by a bird, the crust remaining like a frame.

How long had it been raining, drizzling, that day; easier to calculate than how long since another human being had touched this one with care. It laid itself straight out, unanæsthetized, on the table, for the silvery-cool instruments to dig and chisel into its patient side. The rain, the drizzle, was less than that winter in New York which accumulated liquid and broke in you like the rolling of a river magnified by nostalgia, a river turning over European 'r's. It was less than that; yet under the doctor's metal touch I slept, lulled by the quality of her surgical attention and by the sound de la pluie outdoors.

I wish the ease of sleep had salved you; but the artist being both patient and doctor, you excised, bit by bit, the rosy heart of little things that have genesis in insomnia – the feeling of rotation, the idea of houses – creations, but not always of a kind to be named.

COUNTING SHEEP

	tonguetwisters	the gestes d'un arbre are made of sourcils
		sources jitter
the robust arbuste	take as read	
the standard buisson	take as read	
business of roses	take as read	
	the	
	grain	
a standard rose	chandelier	
a standard lamp	roses from the air	

La serre est trop petite pour les caisses

muffled effect of shears on sheep

oreilles de lapin

tordre tondre

'Nobody can take my style, it is not possible,

at least not for long. do not fret.'

sleep comes in ropes & fruits, pears

                      sleep is initially a stylized form

                      en somme, as we recollect it,

                      flowers are heliotropic

                      dandelion clocks

we cannot grasp the sun – we can grasp a sea urchin

the grand earth-spanning arc of sunrise is fictive, only our calculation

                                makes a globe

three dancing princesses   even astronauts can't

wore out their slippers   completely think about

dancing through the night   the sun

              sooner a prostitute, a driveway, a hedgehog

not-just-doodles because   eye of the hurricane

burqa'd fingerpuppets   sea anemone

                anemometer

                a labyrinth of breezes

           la dame moves   the damier of sleep

           check mate   shah mat

raindrops prelude

mountain

           another &   another square

           earrings, pillow, oreiller

le sentier

a feeling of home rises

from this path, it's an approach; sleep has an architecture with a way in,

                           does insomnia, too,

                           where is the way out?

the eye set well back in a bird's head

exploser exposer plumage & high heels

featherdusted & tumbleweeded   but not to sleep

levitating   sleep is a matter of levitation

                    insomnia fixed on a stick

as if on the beach je joue aux boules

coulante – terrifie

one house is a shaded version of another house

all chemins lead to france

converge, concentric, intersect

le phénix renaît de ses cendres

houses shoot up like lipsticks

the many peaks are plain & tight

'she stepped on a mind'

                    on music paper   qu'elle est le rythme d'une nuit blanche

                                       un sans-papier dans le royaume de l'art

smiley breastbone, sleepless nipples on which closed-mouth

                                       criticisms converge

but how very pretty things are, french girls' hair, a bouquet of

balloons; why don't they float her out

everywhere i carry a sheep across my shoulders, wide peasant stride

'DO   'may   cocoon one self, another

not   I   [banality of a fight, duvet]

disturb' come in'

                    labyrinth   eye centre of its propre labyrinth

                    dirty labyrinths with unruled lines

                    eye becomes an architecture / entravé in its architecture

'Sainte mouton'?   she holds on to the

'Sureté mouton'?   ~~holy~~

'Secrète mouton'?   ~~holy dread which is~~

INSOMNIA MASHUP

Je crois, dur comme fer, au format journal, diary

'the garden notebook, côte-garden of all my houses'

skittles of sleep   stick insect
               skittle insect

mosquito dandelions

Ça ne fait ni queue ni tête but I still love it

      long-stemmed flowers   longer & longer-stemmed flowers

INCANTATIONS

if i can join this mountain & the other mountain, there will be france

cheveluresprécieuses   ifiraisemyarms   whatrainsdown

foracanopy/circus   ifilowermylids   istarttoflower

whensleeplessiimaginepeopleiknowinemblematicpostures

hairscatteredontheshoulders   charming   carriedouttoseaon

turtles'backs

      [have all your dreams in a row]

the cold at the core   sleepless,Iradiatecold   solar,onceagain

must   live   radial

      [give everything away]

      'I Give Everything Away'

Measures of Expatriation — V

Far from Rome

The blue dusk settles at a rate,
and fields can be forgotten
as they are; as-they-were appear
uppermost, lidded, swept smooth;
beneath, left still, kiln-fired
vessels belonging to him,
pleasing to his strong, torn hands –
so very much not in Rome,
this redeployed general.

The sea mixed in your eyes,
arrived at cruel decisions
yet stalling execution.
I would have sworn to die for you
sooner than try to live with you.
The sea swarms in my ears.
I sift your breath through mine.
A modern probe might take me
for less-than-human remains,
for nail-seed dirt and cumin.
I wouldn't mind; being her,
and yours.

        But not in this life –
the intolerable one
which, when the blue dusk scratches,
lends it my eyes. To discern,
alone, your life, indicts me.
Such knowledge a reburial.
Turn me to copper, one of you
gods he only temporized with:
melt me down then score me
the music for last things.

Marginal

An egg is divided
into shell and meat.
When I bent to my task
during the victory visit,
light banged its gongs and passed,
with a travelling step, through me.
I was halves:
yolk and pallor,
brittle and sky,
blankness and savour,
scoop and scorn,
loft and huddle,
core and cry;
was another musician
bare and ashamed
in a yellow slave skirt.
I played hard.
Played wrong.
He stopped in his progress,
for this was his talent:
displaying his goodwill;
impersonal, merciful
latin approbation.
A thrown-cloak equivalent
where we were not Latin
and he was imperial.
Our error, his notes.

Snake in the Grass
for Alaric Hall

My man was menstrual, had fever dreams
of carbonizing metal. In scattering I began:
impure, then piled, twisted, fused,
quenched in oil and sweeter fluids,
my long form agent and symbol
of heavy terror: what it is to be split.
  City of Oxford, you forget little enough
  but rather excel in techniques of diversion and cover.
  City, you have renamed Gropecunt and Slaughter streets;
  driven streams to run their own burials;
  with false surgery, you have sealed
  the wide, one-eyed mercy of a lake
  beneath a car park's sweat, the clang of coins.
  Under Christ Church tower,
  under kings of new history,
  the Jewish town lies in pre-Expulsion sleep;
  under that again, nameless bones.
Do not dishonour me. I am not sleeping.
  Slide your eye back into its drowsy basket.
  Are you alive, when grass is cut,
  to the slip of blades, reptile-quick
  to stain, to twine? Such things
  share my nature: whatever is woven,
  whatever heats up, iridescing with force.
Do not shun me. I am not sleeping.
Glass is the least security. My kind's for re-use,
willing to coil cold in the earth
till each deadly resurrection through your changes of nation,
till your kind hand comes and the smith repairs us.
Slide your eye into the wave and wind of me.
Forget your wife, if you still have one.
The two of us decide who's for the taking.
Bring me to your son, blossoming in his cradle.
Introduce us. I have a name.
Man, join us together. There's wisdom in my core.

Disposal of a Weapon

The sword of Sir Hugh de Morville, one of the four knights who killed Thomas Becket at Canterbury, is thought to have been given to Carlisle Cathedral. A replica of a twelfth-century sword is now on view at Carlisle.

I had to take it somewhere.
   That was the steel.
I took it home.
   That was in stone.
They had to leave it somewhere.
   That was the shell.
The Church stepped in.
   That was in storm.
Steel, stone, shell, storm.

Another Cathedral. Rage rising:
crowds towards us, against our hard work,
Thomas, head split, forcing hearing's gate
with his loud and bloody treasons. Pray
how could I, lacking fluent parlance,
else control them? As clouds address
my hilly sheep in Northumbria?
In a tyrant's robed, balconied words?
With sweets that trade poisons?
                  Visitors,
modern, unburied, probing my rests,
after my doubtless victim's blessing –
also you thoughtless, yet in secret
capitally troubled – that is not
my sword, though something targets your head,
overhangs the roof, disposed to make
short gold of your moment of starred blue.
That is not my sword. We are elsewhere.

Steel, stone, shell, storm.
I, Hugh de Morville,
Lord of Knaresborough,
Honour of Westmorland,
lineal man stamped down
man-killer, saint-maker
by Canterbury history.
Bless or at least excoriate,
do not forget, my name

I know your ancestors without researching them.
You were thick. We were thin. Fast and inaccurate
users of your landscape. Our progress started birds.
We descended, killing in our slenderness. Thick and
thin. Through thick. The thin.
      So far as I was woman,
I despised you in my heart; soon was un-womaned.
Quasi-indistinguishable among willows,
with superior weaponry, we kept on killing,
cried
      what must be victory
                  with curled tongues.
Soon, you stopped sounding wrong.
      Young man, I am older than you think;
why are you sitting next to me? The art of peace:
scribing and diabetes. You bring gold. Thick. Thin.
Like a zoo lion's, your large, unexercised farts;
I inevitably breathe, breathe nearly the same air.

Let's start a conversation. Ask me where I'm from.
Where is home, really home. Where my parents were born.
What to do if I sound more like you than you do.
Every word an exhalation, a driving-out.

To London

It was necessary to move, and at this exit
the beggar, cross-legged at the fork of the tunnel,
calls out *Love*! A welcome, of sorts.
      The night light fucks the suburb
into nightmare familiarity –
not like a shrammed nerd touting
guided walks and histories that contract
imagination for demolition work,
levelling today's housing,
restoring common greens,
lingering at sites orphaned of their fever
hospitals – by no means that hyperliterate,
poor entrepreneur –

It is the view, the barbed wire roaring into view
round and round the playground walltop.
It is the warehouse, warehouse windows blank of occupation.
It is lives, lives supplied in great number,
fulfilment of numbers.
It is the sense of something shared –
the tailor scissors razoring open
fishmouth stitches, the sewn-up pocket
of the new suit,
and finding something –

But it is new, all new,
even the gangs who graffiti chimneys
scrubbed and lovely, deleted
like the railways delete
repeatedly
the head, the occasionally payrolled head,
the feet
of the quartered commuters, of the vertebral week.

Seven Nights in Transit
for Karen Martinez

SATURDAY

'My child.'

The bearded man in the ticket office is calling hardback old women his children. Like the immemorial conversation-killer that Trinidadian parents transmit to their migrant, errant offspring via the newest technologies:

'But you are my child. I can say anything to you. And I can take anything from you. You can say anything to me.'

Like we never moved on. Like sitting watching the notices for cancelled trains at midnight in London when I have to be back in the office first thing on a working Sunday, first thing on what is now the same day as tonight, could be the same kind of misery of waiting as when I was really a child, standing inside the Convent classroom watching the sun shine and wanting to be outside.

It's the other island, it's Trinidad that doesn't move on, isn't it? Trinidad has put on high-rise buildings like we used to put on our mother's gold net high heel shoes and flaming Carnival boots when we were toddlers. But I don't believe the island has changed. Not Trinidad.

The light is narrowing like an eye doctor's slit lamp. *Better this way, or this way?* I can't see. I can't see more than a palm's width. I mustn't sleep in public.

What are you doing here?

SUNDAY

I can only glimpse her though my eyelashes which are sticky with yampee. But those are not my eyelashes. They are coconut trees with ropes knotted to them and planks of wood attached to the ropes, and boys in Sea Scout uniform are measuring the angle of the sun to build their clubhouse with next to no construction equipment, under the direction of the mathematical genius Trini Chinese priest. So we must be in Toco. So this night is taking me to almost equatorial sun, four thousand miles west of England. And when I land, my internal compass-rose flips like my heart and landing in Toco I don't feel that I have travelled west; I feel that we are north-east, on the tip of the island, the original Atlantic island shaped like a boot and which we kicked behind us, growing up.

That crazy lady is looking at me and holding what looks like my handbag. I check myself and I'm not carrying anything. What the hell is this? Since when jumbie does thief? She's not getting away... If I do anything before I die, before I wake, I am going to find out what business it is she has with me. What we have to do with each other.

MONDAY

But I really need to stay awake. Being shut inside this scarcely moving car feels like being shut inside a handbag: the odour of warm leather and straining plastic, the talcum choker of sweat, the lipstick-stained Kleenex tumbling like roses on the floor. The light is not changing. We're stuck in traffic and this is the vagrants' beat; this is where the vagrants beat on rolled-up car windows, their faces like Christ and their crack cocaine limbs too thin to crucify.

It had a goat running up and down the cemetery wall. Man, how I envied the creature its freedom. That was one balanced animal. It knew where it was going, and that nobody was going with it.

The church people left the window louvres open. It still have the Virgin Mary statue, turning her sea-blue back to the street.

The antique shop selling the same garden furniture, cold white-painted iron that used to support hot slave-owning bottoms. The same same garden furniture has been there years now. Like nobody wants it. Like…

Stop it! Damn it! The jumbie lady is in the shop! Why is she crawling on the ground? She thief something else?

Oh my God. I can smell fire.

She is looking at the car, and I can smell burning rubber; I am smelling black history smells, asphalt, molasses, skin, ink and fire.

TUESDAY

I'm telling you I want to go out into the cane field, but there are lines and rows and swooshes of people who all look like *her* and also like my relatives, in this pink room with the grown-up souvenir dolls in glass cases; and every time I try to get up and go out, the people press me back down into the doily-infested armchair. They press gifts into my hands: little bags with sweets and glass bracelets, little books of photos, and I have to be polite, I am that kind of girl. I re-become that child here, on the unchanging island. I have a mysterious and compelling obligation to look at all these little gifts, before I can break through the line of people and go outside. I feel *she* buried *it* in the field. She buried the thing I need to find out about… the thing she didn't exactly steal from me, though I am sure it is mine and somehow it has passed from me; it is part of the past, like *her*, part of the living past; and my country has become another country, and being here always means having left, having left here or being about to leave here, being here is return-

ing to being here and returning surely is about leaving, so this above all
is the place that makes me feel alive-and-dead, it is a birthplace.

WEDNESDAY

If being Trinidadian means travelling with suitcases packed with food
– smuggled sorrel leaves and gallons of ginger beer; entire Christmas
cakes with a poundage like turkeys; saucy doubles that could stain
up your clothes – then I was never Trinidadian. My family were Trini
kitchen traitors. We had a 1970s American cookbook, not a grand-
mother in the countryside; we made pizza, not roti; rissoles, not
dumplings; pinwheel sandwiches, not currant roll. My homesickness
could not be measured out in dashes of Angostura bitters. At the end of
the day, my lonely long-distance-line *good night*s did not scald my lips
like scorpion pepper sauce.

So, although it was very nice and thoughtful of the person who
brought this piece of Trinidad-cake-artist birthday decorative sponge
to London for me, I can't find home in a piece of cake. The piece of cake
is its own sweet home, a construction of icing sugar roses wrapped in
wax paper and tinfoil.

But some ingredient in this cake is drying out my mouth. I am feel-
ing strange. The wind is like... fingers stroking my hair. I wonder what
chemical makes the icing sugar roses so yellow? What a slant the sun
is taking. I never saw it so yellow. Not on this island. Not this island... I
am starting to feel light. Late. Light. Starting to feel too light.

The yellow poui is flowering. That means rain. Will that be enough
to put out the bush fires on the hills?

I want to see it. (I need to find it.) Now while it is flowering; while it
is still light.

Where the yellow poui is flowering, the fire hasn't reached yet on
the hills.

THURSDAY

Take a flower.
Put it there.
Take another flower.
Put it there.
Her hands are full of flowers.
My hands are filled with flowers
Now take the fire. Now.

Ash in the air, pyre on the ground, body in the pyre, camphor on the
tongue.

This is a kindling.
Go away.
Fuck off, they say in England.
Haul your arse.
The body is a garment.
It is burning.
Her hands are empty.
My hands are in her hands.
We are on fire.
Where am I?

FRIDAY

The cathedral is like a forest, and the pillars are like trees. The man in a dress is talking life and death, but I come here for the music. I love the music. I love the trees.

The children are quiet. I can't see which way their feet are going. That lady has a nice dress, too. The shade makes everything here seem kind of violet.

The route taxi taking so long to come. I didn't even know it did stop in the forest.

Last night I dreamt Old Woman and I dreamt Big Snake. What Play Whe you would have bought? I didn't buy anything.

Lady, is how long you waiting for the taxi? Lady? You was already here when I arrive. You here long time?

Oh God. Like she got my number.

My number's up.

Lady, since when you driving taxi?

Let me out.

Here. Here it is.

This is it?

This is it.

Here I am.

Measures of Expatriation — VI

I. THE FAN MUSEUM

This used to be a private house in Scandinavia. It once belonged to a fan collector, who was a great traveller, and was not known to have lived there. There were no signposts to it, although it featured in some listings and I had picked up a brochure for it in a café where there were the most beautiful biscuit tins for sale that I have ever seen, with designs of apples, and a Happy Blonde Lady wig in some coffee-drinker's shopping bag hung on the coat racks at the entrance, for this was summer. Place dissolved, as it tends to do: if the hedge had been less twiggy and the wrought iron more like weaponry, this approach to a stepped doorway via a modest paved path between wildly undimmed replaceable flowers could have been the way into a genteel dwelling in older Port of Spain. I shut up about this, as I tend to do.

(Becoming quieter and quieter so as not to appear to be living in the past: if your friend likes you his eyes will brighten and he will want to drag out fixed explanations of what for you felt like a fleeting reference to a permanent elsewhere that is continuously living and evolving within, in parallel to, and away from you. Call this the norm.)

There was a push-button doorbell but the door was on the latch so I pushed it and peeked in to a very blank hall that was not any tidier than a private house would be if one counted the ghosts of garden scissors and calling cards, stray reprimands and childish outbursts, that dropped dahlia-like into the faintly radiating silence. The ceilings were twice the height of my accustomed English rooms (ssh). A table of dieted elegance, offering more brochures, maintained its poise in an alcove to the right, unpersoned.

(I travel alone so as not to be quiet except by choice: an increase in wordlessness that is not pegged to explanation, like a national currency that has been floated in favour of independent devaluations.)

The doorway into the main space was without a door but blocked by a wrought iron trellis of the kind expected in a conservatory in a black and white film. I edged past it and straightened myself out. This manner of entrance positioned the visitor in such a way that the giant fan appeared side-on, though fully opened. Had I not known that this was the Fan Museum I could have thought that the fan in profile was a crack in a doorway to nowhere, for its side was ebony heavily covered in black lace, and the spread, the thickness of it did not appear. I walked round and looked first at one side, then at the other. It was embroidered with scarlet poppies, corn stalks and vine leaves, on a black background.

The house was narrow: in front of me I could see double glass doors, locked, to a courtyard. To either side were smaller halls with staircases turning steeply to the upper floors of this house that was narrow but winged.

I had a strong, irrational aversion to making a left or right turn. I looked around for a guide to the display, but saw only two identical mirrors in ornate gilt frames on the slightly rounded corners to the left, and a tall, spindly, gilded clock in the right corner, ticking so quietly as to add weight to the silence. The other corner, to the right, had a light patch on the caramel paint, and some protruding metal remains that looked as if a small cabinet had been affixed to the wall just too high for my comfort, at average adult Scandinavian reach. 'Hello!' My voice reverted to a kind of Trinidadian that it had never used in Trinidad: a birdlike screech that would carry over a wrought metal gate (painted orange) across a yard with frizzle fowls and the odd goat.

I quickly went to the left. The room had no windows but two doors at the further corners. These were bolted and locked on the outside. In the middle was an item of furniture like two pine dressers back to back, with many drawers and one or two cupboard sections instead of shelves. I pulled open a hand-width drawer at waist height. Sealed fans were stacked in there like hairbrushes. I felt like an invader and shut it quickly. I reached up to the cabinet knob but decided against opening the door. I opened another drawer at waist height and took out the single fan that was in there. I could not tell if it was sealed or had simply dried shut. It was of light wood and dark lavender paper. Silver-white plum blossom flowered in my mind, but the fan would not open.

My hands started to hurt with the desire to touch or the recollection of touch. They developed a nervous disorder all their own. Something like cramp started to shoot up my arms. My throat and forehead felt hot. I walked around the cabinet and re-crossed the hall of the giant fan. The air seemed exceptionally still. Every one of those fans shut in the possibility of breeze. Every fan existed in the implication of stillness.

(A feeling like being cornered on a veranda in a house in Kingston in an area where the drug barons maintain their beautiful houses, cornered by nothing but the social impossibility of stepping into the street, for these areas boasted a winning safety.)

I went into the right-hand room. There was a bench with a green velvet seat and no fans, and nothing on those two walls. The bench was side on to the door and side on to a portrait facing the door. If life-sized, this portrait was of a tall man who had the shape but not the years of youth and who was turned three-quarters away. His back was bent and shaded across the shoulders as if by the habit of paying painstaking attention. This could have been his main form of love. Instead of getting up, I turned my head to look at the picture. The bench was, unusually, exactly the right height for me.

When it grew dark I thought that it might be time to take the latch off the front door and lock it. I have been laughed at for sleeping like a statue. (It is more yogic and less static; with the spine at full stretch, the lungs can excavate the air. (Ssh.)) Now sleep emerged from the borders of the body like a well-trained force whose first, long-ago, unworded battle was with their own tentativeness and who therefore show little hesitation advancing into alien terrain. First my feet folded one on to the other, soles partly touching; the seams of my legs twisted and relaxed, clasped into position like an enchanted dress gone back into a nutshell. My arms did the same and even my ribs felt as if semi-detached like a purring cat's. I was shutting up. My eyelids shuttered. Under my tongue a word tucked itself like the head of a bird under its wing and my hair curtained the face like a blackout blind over the copper pagoda bird cage.

The sleep voice in my head was a clear murmur. What a coincidence, how productive of accidents it might have been if at that moment I had heard his name!

I was glad to visit the Museum of Fans.

II. THE GOD OF OBSTACLES

Expatriation: my having had a *patria*, a fatherland, to leave, did not occur to me until I was forced to invent one. This was the result of questions. The questions were linked to my status elsewhere. Transferring between elsewheres, I had to lay claim to a somewhere, sometimes a made-up-on-the-spot somewhere. Gradually this Trinidad began to loom. Then it acquired detail. I never have returned home to it, though, not to the place that I have had to hear my own voice describe when in conversation with the Priests of the God of Obstacles, they who wield the passport stamps. This luxury of inattention, invention, and final mismatch... a 'Trinidad' being created that did not take my Trinidad away (my Trinidad takes itself away, in reality, over time)... that is expatriation, no? An exile, a migrant, a refugee, would have been in more of a hurry, would have been more driven out or driven towards, would have been seeking and finding not.

If the Schengen Agreement had been a person, it would have been old enough to join the army, drive, vote, marry, have a proper job, be punished in serious ways for serious offences, all this and also have a gap year before going to a carefully selected non-Oxbridge university, in its own countries. It would not have been nearly as old as I was, when I applied for a visa according to its rules. It was a whippersnapper. I would not have dated it. It was ordering me around.

Trips home to Trinidad folded neatly into trips home to the UK. My aeroplane was a double-headed snake belting across the Atlantic. Now, as a graduate student, I started to think about travelling. I had been going back home to Trinidad at every possible opportunity. My father, in Trinidad, was very ill, as he had been ever since I had known him. In my early twenties, I realized that this illness was not going to change except gradually to get worse. In some ways this realization was freedom. I started looking to cross other waters.

I had almost enough proof to satisfy the Schengen authorities that I could apply for a tourist visa: being in full-time education, the co-owner of a family house, and in a permanent relationship with a native-born UK citizen so blond, athletic and well-spoken in more than one language that he frequently was mistaken for a German. Almost enough proof.

Hopping off from Oxford to spend a spontaneous few days in Munich, I only had to book and pay for my flights and get my other half to wheedle a formal letter of invitation from the Stiftung Maximilianeum (he was on an exchange scheme there; they didn't know me). Oh yes, and just rustle up a few other documents, all perfectly reasonable: evidence of accommodation for the duration of the stay, declaration of ports of arrival and departure and borders to be crossed: before ringing the automated visa line and getting an appointment six weeks or so in advance of travel. Lastminute.com travellers, eat your hearts out! Who can complain when everything is planned? Proof sufficient had I given: it was no dream of mine to quit my DPhil at Christ Church to sell oranges in the streets of Europe or, perhaps, travel with a donkey, like R. L. Stevenson, or with a circus, like Robert Lax, or with a notebook, like a young man with a ~~white shirt black poloneck~~ recycled half-zip fleece and a flair for poetry. Thus was I saved from turning into a travel writer. Unease is relative.

Obtaining the visa was no great shakes. My other half accompanied me to the German Embassy's hall-style waiting room. The Wielder of the Passport Stamps, plump with brown fondant hair, melted sweetly at our cross-cultural devotion. His many blushing nods embellished the ceremony of passport-stamping. He did not so much dismiss as bow

away our case. This happy send-off carried me into the aloneness (I
was alone most of the time) of being appreciably foreign (but in a nice
way) in Munich. In the early mornings I took the air in the Englischer
Garten. Large men with baying hounds bounded out of the mist and
hollered greetings largely. I camped out on a guest bed in the Stiftung
Maximilianeum, in a room stacked with nineteenth-century copies of
the *Pall Mall Gazette*. Some mornings I limbered up with a swim in the
basement pool of the Stiftung, which also housed the Bavarian Par-
liament. A single parliamentarian might be wallowing determinedly
across it. Again there would be the greeting, this time something like
'Well swum!' Without functional German and determined not to speak
English, I tactlessly negotiated my way in French throughout streets
and markets, and was given a handful of free postcards for no discerni-
ble reason at an art exhibition where the gallerist took a non-predatory
shine to me. Whereas the Alice in Wonderland porters at the Oxford
college where I read for my BA, MSt and DPhil with few exceptions
challenged me at the college gate several times a week in a sudden
fit of misperceiving me as a tourist (my floaty hot pink shirt was the
trigger), the Parliamentary guard at the entrance to the Stiftung only
failed to recognize me on one occasion. The minute I gave the Stiftung
guard a big smile and pointed up at the window of the room where I
was staying, he looked genuinely remorseful for running at me with
his gun and shouting; he acknowledged our shared embarrassment
with a shy All's Clear.

In springtime I thought of travelling from Germany to Italy. My other
half would be there on another exchange. With disbelief he witnessed
my insistence on looking up the paperwork for such a land of sun-
light. A fault line appeared in our communications. Why did he not
understand? I was spontaneously attempting to cross a border! Being
from a small island, I was historyless (perhaps three friends bothered
to remember that I had a family background) yet I could not live up to
anyone's hope of finding a malleable girl dropped from the sky. Paper-
work stuck to me, like the paper slippers shredded on the feet of a
fairytale person setting off on a highway of glass. I heaped myself for
hours into the seats at the relevant building in Munich. Eventually, all
was clear. This stamp was diamond-shaped.

Sick on the train with gin and disagreements till the air seemed yellow
and accursed, I felt nightmarish unsurprise when the people with the
printed list arrived in our carriage. They were checking passports. They
were not sure that Trinidad was a country, though the visa itself looked
all right. Some strange blindness seemed to strike them as they looked
at the list. Trinidad was not on the first page; the second page had an
apparent heaviness or stickiness, it would not more than half turn...
What god of obstacles was moving in these officials? My then other

half addressed them Germany. I was curiously sidelined; eye contact was not made, verbal contact seemed not possible. In that moment of sidelining, the god of obstacles visited the passport controllers differently, and the name Trinidad manifested itself on their printout.

I tried to trace what shocked me in the momentary non-existence of my smaller island. To my horror, it was that I felt they should have heard of it because... because... I reposed a trust in cricket and football (games which for me fulfil two conditions of storybook romance: I admire but do not understand them) to put us on the map. I secretly did not credit our Nobel laureate(s) with making us known usefully, for example to people who checked lists in trains. I interrogated myself further and uncovered an amoral willingness to locate Trinidad geographically with reference either to tourism in Barbados or the American invasion of Grenada, possibly both, according to nothing more than what I could guess of my interlocutor's likely interests. The important thing was to convince the list-holder that my country existed sufficiently to deserve to be looked up. How things have changed: nowadays a mention of Venezuela should be enough.

The god of obstacles stayed quiet during some years in which young Schengen and I politely ignored each other. Though having caused my British citizen too much perplexity for our attachment to endure, I was myself a British resident and had a real job at Girton College, Cambridge: I was spoken for, on letter-headed paper. I could queen it over your lists.

But the gods have a way of raising the game. This was in a year when, all my papers in order, I was about to leave Florence, independent and blithe. The young official who took my passport got a look of handsome stupidity. He scrutinized the flora and fauna that bedeck the Trinidad coat of arms. He burst out laughing, waving for a female colleague to come over. He pointed at my passport and muttered something to her. Now they both were laughing. (They looked so young.) It was half an hour before the plane was due to take off. No list of countries was in evidence.

In Italian that was vestigial, nervous, overcourteous, I asked what was the matter. Oh do not raise the question of *the role of the decorative arts in border control situations, or, never judge a passport by its cover*! That was, however, veritably the question. The stupid, handsome face stopped laughing. Hands gambled the passport open on random pages. The Wielders of the Stamps could not let me out of Italy. Why? Because I had a Schengen visa, yes, they could see that (it spreadeagled across a page), but I had no visa for the UK.

I gently moved the pages to show the permit that granted my right to residency in the UK. It did not cross my mind to try to explain the concept 'Commonwealth', though as a Commonwealth citizen I could anyway have entered the UK for a limited period without a visa. Two years' university tutoring had taught me how to recognize pretend-reading pretty fast. These Wielders of the Stamps were just pretending to read the British residency permit.

Alas, the words were all they had: the British permit consisted of a meanly inked text, with no translation into another European Union language. Confusingly, the wording referred to 'leave' rather than 'permission', and 'indefinite' rather than 'permanent'. Leave? Go? Was this something saying I should stay away from the UK for a while? Tradition, not marketing, certainly not machine translatability, must have been the force governing the choice of words.

Working in the airport of a major tourist destination not a million miles from Albion, the two young people appeared both unfamiliar with and utterly uncomprehending of this official sign. Worse yet, the stamp was lacking, was intrinsically unconvincing: it featured no coronet, no rolling waves, no rose, thistle, lion, unicorn, oak, beef, or albatross... I promptly affected dismay. What an ugly permit! How British, I cried disloyally; not a single picture! But do you mean you don't know Trinidad? It is a beautiful island! You must visit! The beaches are brilliant, the sea is so blue! We are very friendly! We love visitors! Why have you never visited? But Italy is so beautiful too! Oh, I see I don't know why there are no pictures for the permit but that is what the British have done!

I continued my Ministry of Tourism spiel in between rendering the meanly inked text word for word as best I could, till the Wielders of the Stamps stopped me. I sprinted on to the plane.

Did a deeper disloyalty reside in my touristification of Trinidad, which could make itself imaginable to my conversationalists only through me, or in my mock-criticism of my adoptive Britain, whose white-cliffed reputation could outface whatever I had to say?

Expatriate, I had acquired the confidence to hurtle into having to start over. It was a way of going on.

How was it that till questioned, till displaced in the attempt to answer, I had scarcely thought of myself as having a country, or indeed as having left a country? The answer lies peripherally in looming, in hinterland; primarily in the tongueless, palpitating interiority. Trinidad was. Trinidad is. In the same way, some confident speakers do not think of themselves as having an accent. They will say so: 'I don't have an accent! You have an accent!' In those accentless voices compass points spin, ochre and ultramarine flagella fling themselves identifiably towards this that or the other region. It is a motile version of that luxury, solidity, non-reflectivity that is the assumption of *patria*. So different is the expat from the refugee, who has her country on her back, or the migrant, who has countries at his back.

What would I have called home, before I began creating home? Before I had to learn to ravel up longitude, latitude, population, oil rigs, mobile phone masts, prayer flags, legality of fireworks, likely use of firearms, density and disappearance of forests, scarlet ibis, other stripes of scarlet, into a by-listeners-unvisited, communicable, substantial image of 'Trinidad'?

Language is my home. It is alive other than in speech. It is beyond a thing to be carried with me. It is ineluctable, variegated and muscular. A flicker and drag emanates from the idea of it. Language seems capable of girding the oceanic earth, like the world-serpent of Norse legend. It is as if language places a shaping pressure upon our territories of habitation and voyage; thrashing, independent, threatening to rive our known world apart.

Yet thought is not bounded by language. At least, my experience of thinking does not appear so bound.

One day I lost the words *wall* and *floor*. There seemed no reason to conceive of a division. The skirting-board suddenly reduced itself to a nervous gentrification, a cover-up of some kind; nothing especially marked. The room was an inward-focused container. 'Wall', 'floor', even 'ceiling', 'doorway', 'shutters' started to flow smoothly, like a red ribbed tank top over a heaving ribcage. Room grew into quarter. Room became segment. Line yearned till it popped into curve. The imperfections of what had been built or installed: the ragged windowframe or peeling tile: had no power to reclaim human attention to 'floor' or 'wall' as such. Objects were tethered like astronauts and a timid fringe of disarrayed atmosphere was the immediate past that human activity kept restyling into present. The interiority of the room was in continuous flow. *Wall, floor* became usable words again in a sort of silence.

I had the sense to shut up about the languageless perception. Procedure for living.

Language is my home, I say; not one particular language.

IV. WORD BY WORD

Do you know that party or family game where each person says the first word that comes to mind, prompted by what the person before has just said? Outrages and banalities and brilliancy link up at high speed, a wedding dance of animated paperclips. I have not been able to play that game. It induces hesitation and something like a stammer. 'Don't think! You're thinking!' – a telling-off from the party dictator. Often the uttered word would summon up another word in a totally inappropriate register or language; more often, several words at once, in a kind of bee dance; most often, no word at all: sounds and images surged up, and I searched to find something to keep the game going. But this was not an expat phenomenon. This happened in Trinidad, too, before my move to the UK. Perhaps it was a hypersensitization to the fluidity and zigzagging of Trinidadian speech, where flowery translations of Sanskrit and the formality of the older Christian (mostly Catholic) liturgies naturally mix into the same track as the tricksy shrug and bread-and-curses everydayness of Spanish-French-Portuguese-Syrian-Chinese-Scottish-Irish-(English)? Was everyone else pretending to have one-word events in their brain, while secretly choosing from a *retentissante* horde?

Expatriate.
Exile.
Migrant.
Refugee.

V. A RECORD OF ILLEGITIMATE REACTIONS

A record of illegitimate reactions... If these words: expatriate, exile, migrant, refugee: turned up in the children's game, what, on the instant, would be my wordless upsurge?

Refugee. Severity of the olive green cover of the J.S. Bach *Preludes & Fugues* book that was my master such long hours of my teens. Flight and the intricacy of flight and a scrambling to be heard and but a coming together in the end. *Refugio.* A cavern. Mary and Joseph, straw in a rough box? Promise of a place. Higher up than a stable and more difficult of access. A path to fall off, a lorry underside to grip to. The arrival another unpacking. The station, built or unbuilt, ever inadequate, dark and cavernous. People with fine features and ripped feet fetching water with difficulty to a place of non-recognition. *Refugee* should have been, in Trinidad, the Guyanese maids; the Asian East African doctors; the Sindhi shop-owners, plumped under the new sun but with an unspoken... fear?... a *having-feared* behind eyes browner than mine, working the sharp-edged wordbatch WAR to WARES. A too-late identification. For they were not *refugee*, not to the mind of the child in the word-game. Refugee had flight in it and fleeing to a huddle of wrongness; a translation into a community of incommunicability. There is brown and mid-blue, blister-purple, love-scarlet and a great deal of black in this word. There is the insistence on losing and finding, finding and not having, a home.

No, not that.

Migrant. Migrant geese or some such was where first I heard the word so as to note it, the word migrant actually not alone at origin, part of a phrase with white wings, and it is driven it is thoughtless it is magnetically on course steered by stars and obsessed with diving for food and likely to have secreted in its braincoils a chart for the way home. A cyclical, undependable word – a trait prettifying itself when observed by the other species whose skies it occupies – Migrant is all the birds of the air and I lack the balance to set off on a flight with a due destination and a warm or frosted prompting back. Migrant is cerulean and khaki and it has a lot to say for itself once encamped temporarily by a river that will do. All movement, this word. Out at elbows or tense-thighed: verbal. Absolute: adjectival. In the singular, it implies plurals: migrant isolate in so far as rising from or surrounded by settlers. The hunted, hunter, unconcerned.

No, not that.

Exile. Exile is Joseph. Exile is Moses. Exile is a boy or a man and sand and serpents. Exile is Sri Rāma. Exile is a pair of sandals on the throne for your brother will not rule in your place while you have been kept from your kingdom and have gone into the forest. Exile is an ancient song. Exile is melismatic. Exile is flattened in English. *Exil* in French is yet more clipped: *exil* is a short step from death; it is St-Ex, St-Exupéry crashed into the desert, or the pilot's verray corporeal assumption into his beloved night, wind, sand and stars. Sable encore. Exile has a grain to it. *Exilio, esilio* is one to call from mountain tops. It is a maker of songs who can make vowels from objects, a ram's horn, a conch shell; and I think he is male again, sinewy and unbathed for weeks on end without minding, expecting his songs to be transmitted, and when he arrives somewhere he will know how to make a fire and cook but someone else will bake the bread for him. Fire is in exile and the word burns me so I cannot use it; it is an hysterical word, I shall weep

and do wrong to others in order to avenge somebody if I think hard enough about exile, a bed of scorched earth and somebody I was in love with in a dream. Exile, a constant series of disruptive transactions between resignation and prophecy. Exile is a Book of Books. Exile is a find by someone else and the bones chitter the story, so every interpretation, being late, is haunted and warped into footnotes around the song. Exile, renewer of membranes. A sweated blanket of footnotes and departed feet. I picked it up and its black and white pattern began bleeding most deeply into my appalled, osmotic hands.
No, not that.

Expatriate. *Non dépaysée, sin saber por qué ni por qué sé yo, unhousèd free condition.* I arrive at the theme, which surely is a citation. I am incited to pluck out the heart of the mystery. I am transported on the instant to another century. *Patria* sings an Italian tenor. No expiry, please.

All Your Houses
Notebook Including a Return
for Andre Bagoo

As if no thought beyond immediate transferral: mind to paper.

I

Next door there are workmen. The tenants have been disposed of; disappeared, perhaps, into the television sets that go on and stay on all along the road. Life has never so much resembled a drama of nothing. Men with special knocks introduce themselves, not by their names, in deep, uncertain voices. And nearly nightly, in just the one embarrassment of a house that knoweth not curtain tassels, is the blue, white and red 2 a.m. festival. 'Honest, officer, I never would have done something like that.' 'I can chastize my daughter in any way I want.'

Next door the workmen are converting the loft. So far they have punched five holes in our wall. Daylight was visible through one hole, now covered over with something like silver foil. Bricks in Trinidad were red to the core. These houses have grey bricks, grey on the inside, dust falling through grey.

The workmen next door explained that they have not been careless. Walls are expected to be six to eight inches thick. These are four inches at best, built for Victorian replaceable grateful people. The thing that is constantly constricted in my head eases a little, now the house on one side shows up its shoddiness. It feels less stuck together; not sweated so thick with aspirational, windowgazing, briefly guttering lives. The imposition of this house feels more impersonal, like rain.

The nervous chatter of minds not yet forming themselves into poems: not to inflict that on friends...

II

All winter the heating had been fixed. The college workmen came to the house and stuck the heating at 'on' with a screwdriver. April, and they were fixing it again.

That character (whose?), that superstition: scissors snipping the air provokes or presages conflict. Air is likened to paper. Air and paper are full of voices.

Always to drift off alone, in a house where another is already sleeping: how to take down the crazy scaffolding of words, arrive at ground level, and maintain the illusion of companionship into the alien land of sleep?

The end of the page is where the line stays drawn for good.

III

This college is gutted. A road owned by another college passes through this college. Why are those buildings so blank a presence? They curve or slope about green space. Their solidity resembles refusal, perhaps the refusal to speak. Shapes cast in concrete from a French formal garden magnified a hundred times: at snail's height I enter, without a sense of entrance; un-entranced. Leather and darkness inside spite the glass. So strange triumphs cover for the absence of beauty and age.

Whereas in the moneylaundering banks on the other side of the ocean, where half-private waiting rooms are cousin to these teaching rooms, there were families who sat about while their heads went off into truly obscure interiors, here are first names and no heads and nowhere private to go. Conversation lounged around shared intentions: all these families would visit Disney World. Conversation lounges around shared ambitions: but I am not on the same page.

Morning had trembled awake. The first similar shakiness moved a long cold finger down my left arm from shoulder to fingertips, stretching a nerve, taking years to pass off. I had lifted the box with the Christmas tree over the Convent gate. It would have been easy enough to walk around a little way, to another gate, not kept locked. It was inconvenient that this gate should be locked. I wanted it open. I wanted to lift.

Shakiness is visible in cramping as I try to hold the pen; I do not trust myself with speech, though the inside of my head is somewhat recognizable.

IV

The basement is orange, pillarbox red, and poster paint blue. I was not conceived or thought of in the 1950s, though I have seen town houses painted in the 1990s, set aside by local councils in the south of England for well-meaning things to happen indoors in an underfunded way. This basement, however, is dedicated to the reading of poetry. Two blackboards make the wall loud behind the reader. Whoever reads whatever will have to stand in front of a cool message bullying people to be slower. I elasticate time.

The Hercules complex: name and define it? The certainty of being strong and somehow at fault. The inability to cope with others' performance of hurt. The existence as a marvellous witness who puts the seal on the confession that it is someone frailer who has full humanity.

That book they are talking about was written to give the feeling of thinking to people who fear the habit of reflection. It is very good. I do not think that it was good for me. The backs of chairs are rearranging themselves into arch wooden animals. Every fiction bends into the document of a writing experience. Every word appears as a proper name.

No kindness to one's own mind is possible in this process, which must not stop for theirs.

V

The workmen continue to hammer the walls next door. This is no call to start the day. Whether they do their job is quite separate from whether I do mine. The morality of pure disconnectedness makes the easy poetry of analogy impossible. My face is dirty and my black fleece is stained with tea and I am hopeless at knitting and sewing.

There were his attempts to pull me back with hurt eyes and soft words from the 'terrible distance between us'. There was her research on the Easter Vigil: in the dark, lightening, northern-hemisphere days leading up to the celebration, church bells were not rung or were rung with wooden clappers – dumb bells, during the ages when so little else rumbled the foundations, stirred the sky, discomposed the soundscape. There was another one talking of a rich eastern country, an architect father, and a building like a white sail with ripples in it. So I talked to yet another one, about my tulips and about his chickens; about his chickens eating his tulips; about his having an egg sandwich made from his chickens' eggs; about his having no intention to eat his chickens.

Then the poets read. A fascination was exercised through them. People came up to them, wanting something not human: sympathy untroubled by the need for explanation; the most secret imaginings anticipated; an answer to the terrible, purely internal manifestations of love, which had them walking about whole but gutted.

For a perfect reader, invulnerable to extravagances.

The man next to me on the ten-hour flight has insomnia. His white clothing is in layers, and neat. He repacks his hand luggage, which is full of gifts. He was an athlete who represented his nation. Injury and necessity sent him to the factory near Croydon to make plastic cups. He is too big to ignore, even if he had not confided to me his fear of the losses that night shifts make in his mind. The art of memory becomes a topic of discussion. Will his family remember him? His trip is a secret. The plan is to take a taxi and stop part way up the road from the family business (a bar), stroll in, and ask to buy a drink... I wonder, I wonder. Recognition: can it happen? Can a family survive it?

The postcards that I sent to England from Trinidad may not arrive in England until after I have returned there myself. The hand-made shoe cupboard in the house formerly known as 'home' contains a pair of gold mules. Everyone disavows owning them. I wear them. My toes are empurpled.

Four thousand miles traversed and there is a workman in the neighbourhood. He talks, saying the same thing again and again. The hundred dollars – sixty dollars that 'she' would make him pay for food, because she does not like 'black people'. He emits a soft wordless murmur in between the statements, seeking agreement from his invisible someone. He stops his complaint with a final murmur, grievance winding down. Closer to me than the place where he works and complains is the yard where a little frog makes round sounds at night.

An old woman should not have to stand outside any door, calling; stand there giving reasons why it is all right to talk through the door. – Didn't you also spend the night lying miserably awake? – No, I grab sleep when I can.

VII

The wind is lifting and sinking in that preparatory way. The curtains closed, the iron-grilled windows glassed-in: yet the heaviness in the body registers the likelihood of a downpour. The door slams. I must make time. Apparently no-one is there. In the air-conditioned boudoir, the two older women continue their reminiscences. What was the real name of that man from their youth: and was he the man who killed someone and went to jail, or the one with one arm whose arm was bitten off?

The friends from the other side of the world visit in dreams. I dreamt her in a quite imaginary flat, ghastly-faced and looking more like Sylvia

Plath than like herself. She told me that she had had nothing to eat but a bowl of soup for the last ten days, although she was pregnant. I know that city well on foot, unlike my 'home' town. But the dream broke up the streets: the supermarkets became small and far away, the takeaways reverted to their locations of one and two decades before. I could not work out what to choose from their menus that would make our loved ones agree to join us.

The two older women remembered the three-legged dog named 'Tripod'; the man with arms different lengths, nicknamed 'Clock'; the one-eyed man (bigger) who was 'Polyphemus' and the one-eyed bus conductor (smaller) who was 'Cyclops'. – But the bus conductor, would he have known what he was being called? – Yes, that story was in the elementary school primer.

British (Scottish, Irish, French, Spanish (education)) was best. Time passes.

VIII

Sitting at lunch on the other side of the world that day, he refused to hear of the unkindness of poetry. – Sitting at the foot of a mountain, trying to describe by smartphone how precipitous it is, to a friend who has never left the valley, nor felt gradient's drag inside toiling muscle-and-bone. – Being stranded on a desert island for six hours, knowing that it is only for six hours, but that during that time there is no recourse, you are truly stranded and can only look out at the sea, or do something such as can be done on the island. – Tell me about the fisherman who visits an aquarium on his day off?

'Pig Devours Swineherd'. That was from the front page of this national paper, once. There are news stories that you remember as if they were dreamt. The details have passed into dream. Was it that the couple was sitting on the sofa in their living room, watching television, the night the truck careened off course, blundering through their garden wall, over the garden, into the wall of the house, and so ran them over while they were seated in their living room? Since then I like to say that it's safer not to stay indoors. There have been other reasons for saying so.

The car overturned on the highway. The parents were safely inside. She, confused, went along and across the highway, seeking help. Hit by a car, she was run over by three others, none of which stopped, as her parents watched. I cannot picture this. As I hear of her, I see instead a troop of horses galloping and rising to jump over a human body so that it will not be trampled as they pound on their way. I seem to see this

in midair from a narrow and shifting plane between the road and the
rising hooves of the horses: bared herbivore teeth, red sand flying, and
sweat on the blood bay and chestnut coats.

The thought of the thing has me in a lock, refusing to be thought; sense-
lessly and as if throning in a place set for it, the image displaces the
unthought.

IX

A thousand little ways of showing confused concern to the woman
with no child and no paying job: I have seen and can chant the avatars
of kindness. The idea of writing is triviality or madness. On the other
side of the world, there is fierce competition for an academic post. –
Literature. Well, I'm glad you like it. (Spoken weakly.) – Am I allowed
to invent the term *paraliterature*? (For this is what so many work on,
when all must be published.) Tea is the solution, here as there.

A thousand little comforts on this side of the world, utterly lacking in
the other: from the extra room for the gods to the high-speed broad-
band and the men who craft new kitchens from questionably garnered
teak, I have benefited and wondered. – Why do the children keep play-
ing jail? Small holes in the lawn are dug, not to meet a friend in China
nor yet to create lakes, but as traps for bad men. The study door is
slammed on imaginary people, who have been bad and must be kept
in until they get good and can be let out. The getting good was the
grown-up modification to the shooting game. Do we know anyone in
jail? No, hardly even some of the people who might have put them
there. That should not be so interesting.

Sunlight on the other side of the world brings the real citizens out in
droves, pale blue and bumpy and too pleased for words. Unreal citizen:
I find no surprises in sunlight, however rare its intensity. Sunlight taps
in to a sense of the prolongation of time. It is not even a return to a
norm. It is that there must be more of it. Now it has begun. Similarly,
on this side of the world, enclosure. I overreact to small intervals of
enclosure, as if the endlessness of what used to be home, with locks
and standards and illness, could begin again.

What was the week like, earlier? I seem to be missing Thursday and can't
reconstruct it.

'As idle as a painted ship upon a painted ocean'. A pleasure to be pressed between flat sea and flat sky into the two-dimensional glisten. A pleasure in the horizon as a lost line of pure waiting. The pleasure is not in the repetition; is it in the suspense? 'O love, be fed with apples while you may': May is itself a while. Apple-blossom time. – Do not speak my name in a beggar's tone.

We went to the mangrove. I lack the heart to record the cheerful practical banter in the boat. 'I could lend thee obscureness now, and say / Out of myself, there should be no more day, / Such is already my felt want of sight.' The silky anteater was asleep, and they woke it. Being in its natural habitat, it was on show.

It was the child's first visit to this cousin. Standing solemn on the red tiles, he said that the antique Chinese horses should have motors added to make them go. Then people could ride them. A bat got into the room. Someone went after it with a squash racket. I stood by the swimming pool and chirruped. It found the way and flew off into the sunset.

To practise withholding, being here without being here, keeping people waiting and their love at arm's length, is to be undeserving of written space. – She was pumping you! What do you know about her? – From the other side of the world: How is the trip, apart from the exotica? – To think up something to write to them; to be read by them; to have their words…

XI

My mother's family comes from the East: from the East of Trinidad: Sangre Grande. The source of stories of fear and of pragmatism shifts the mind East. The second youngest girl recalls the praying mantis. The beads of its eyes clicked over and over. She was held in terror. She had gone to fetch a cardboard box for cricket-wicket and this thing was indoors wringing and locking and switching the ends of its forelegs, like the itch of restraint. In terror she hit out. It began to move its legs and wings as if to attack her. She went. The terror stayed. The youngest girl recalls the anaconda. As if casually, Trinidad, sedimentary, no coral spit, once broke off from Venezuela. Mainland-sized animals with nonstandardized names roam the island state. The houses were respectable and wore wooden lace, stepping high above their own yards. Chickens ran freely, but for one that was in the coils of an anaconda. My grandfather, a gentle bright-eyed man who could shoot seabirds out of the air, killed the snake with one shot. Before

anyone could throw away the carcass of the bird, a woman came up.
She said that there was nothing wrong with the fowl. She took it home
and cooked it.

Why in a conversation with someone who is not well and asks me – Do
you believe in God? do I say – No, not really, when at other times to
other people I say and mean that I believe in *gods*?
Why does she look at me without much surprise while telling me that
like all atheists I am on the path to the devil and that my name will be
forgotten after I die?
Why does my name being forgotten make me think not of being prayed
for but of literary records and the traces of their destruction?
Why when she told me how much time she spent praying for people, in
detail, did I think – that must take very long?
Why did she bestow a social embrace on a damned person?
Why did I promise her to read the Bible?
Why did I think – it is context?

The grown-ups, not far away, are playing Scrabble. Three children
under the age of five are on the sofa. I am sitting with the children. The
television is on. The eldest asks – Why is the man on the road dead?
Three pairs of similarly carved eyes turn their luminosity on me.
The second eldest says – I know what is die! It is going to the hospital
and staying a long time.
Three pairs of eyes.
I say – No. It's not always like that. It's usually more like going to sleep.
Everyone dies. Many people die when they are old.
The man on the road on the news may or may not have been one of
the bandits who died in a shootout near the airport. They were shot
after throwing a hand grenade through the window of a policeman's
car. The car went up in flames. The policeman, whose nickname was
'Police', died. He happened to be a friend of the family.
Three pairs of eyes resume their childishness, one stage further on.

*To be looked at as if one is neutral ground. To identify with the narrative
voice when one reads novels. To have no child in a house where the women
are women together. What about the instantaneous alerts of kindness?
What about belly dancing? Salmon strips of light in the sky? The saffron
ceremony at night in the river? Is it true that the growth curve of fish never
plateaus out? What would it mean to live with the flame turned low? What
is the freedom of thought enshrined in the constitution if the evening con-
stitutional is a few paces for the remote control? – Why do you want to live
over there? – Because I can walk around at night on my own. – But why you
want to walk around at night on your own?
To be looked at as if one is neutral ground...*

This the wrong reaction. When, in the country where I walk around alone, there is a night of men singing about Pakis, I do not feel that they are singing about me: my ancestors left South Asia before the partition of India. When the men, having passed my house, change their singing to a theme of detailed lust, singing about women, I do not feel that they are singing about me. One of the neighbours must be the woman: I have become the Paki. When the singing men stop and call out that they are not disturbing the peace, I wonder whether they are reassuring each other, or whether they have encountered someone walking around alone, perhaps from the direction of the park with understood gaps in the railings. This is the wrong reaction: instead of accepting the place of theme, to continue thinking like audience...

At the tortoise race, the tortoises are placed inside a ring of lettuce leaves. The winner makes its way first to the food. This was English summer, laced with strawberries and cream and Icelanders who had flown south, bearing gifts of a spatula and a pancake pan. Across the black water, on the whitepink coral sand, there are no winners in crab races, though a winner is picked. There is also no lettuce. Crabs run anyhow.

Who has no relatives? In Iceland there was a man who was known as the Night Stalker. He used to break into people's houses at night. That was when for the first time people started keeping their balconies locked. Before they didn't have to, even in Reykjavík. Mostly he just walked around people's houses and flats in the night, looked at them sleeping and so on. Eventually they caught him. – The brother of a friend of a friend started going out with a girl. She introduced herself like this: – I am the sister of the Night Stalker. Apparently that had become the way she introduced herself.

Like you drop from the sky or what? Spoken word. Sped arrow. To speak to those who do not read you. To flee from the space that remains clear inside the head so long as writing is the continuity.

XIII

Half a crown of sonnets – Love is like religion – You – your real voice – You – the real you – Come – Obsession drives the mind. So its language bends to music. Laughter slips beneath the form that's fixed. But it is a short form. Things that are long and twisting and compendious see the half a crown dropped by the wayside. Things that are monolithic from a distance and in detail uncontained are of the future. They have no place in the va-et-vient of this sequence, not belonging to the alternate staccato and legato here-and-now.

Blue lightning last week and this week the modem fizzled, the telephone line is dying and coming to life again, the fridge has stopped working and our food been transferred to a shared fridge a mile and a half away up an oak staircase with no lift, insomnia kicked in, a fourteenth-century man in black sits in green light under the city council hollies, the editor adds a final exclamation mark in distrust of the manuscript ardency of a lover out in the cold, the milk is delivered by a milk float and the milk bottles along the road are smashed till the gutters pearl with it, one friend is with child and cheerful on crutches with her pelvis coming apart, one has invested in hamsters that can be heard pedalling through the night, one lies on the gravel watching air balloons and talking ancient Greek and Brooklyn, one eats doughnuts at the fun fair in a pleased yet morose fashion, one reports snobbery about poetry vs. texts, one is forced at times to take supplements of praise for the small-but-perfectly-formed poems of yet another witty, erotic woman poet who literarily guts fish. – You have such a rich life over there, you know, you are privileged. Don't worry about coming home. – Cannot gut fish.

And another friend like the loveliest kind of pencil, faintly scented with wood, inscribed with gilt, sharp yet giving. The rest of them told us that they were going to another party so we got up eagerly and went outside. None of them got up. They were comfortable in the pub. Sober and tired we stayed outdoors, waiting without looking in or looking up, and wondered why so many good rain poems were in French, when it was English weather. The English weather rained down on us until we realized that we were standing beneath the hanging baskets that had just been watered so that the plants could have their evening drink without risk of evaporation.

The rule of silence. Flooding one's friends. Small rain. Efficiency sufficient to effect happiness. Enforced rest.

XIV

For normality to be a record of tension. To wake every morning with clenched teeth. For sleep to be wearing teeth down. To be aware of the boundaries of your face from the ache and pressure of a jaw that has been gritted. For the undoing that lengthens. To have a clenched face and eyes shaded under and therefore to resemble these crowds.

The book by a man who had been in the revolution and who created an unlikeable character who tagged along after the revolutionaries with scraps of paper in his bag is now set for examinations. Other places not being a host of people in dust-coloured clothing, nor blue and orange fabric that was a bundle once tied with care, nor yet a woman with a burning face and a child on her shoulder, still not the trek over the mountain pass that perhaps for centuries had demarcated distance, border, that which must not be crossed lightly, the impassable, The End, why are there not better warnings when the mood descends, the failure of patience with poets who write after watching the news? This is not a stanza.

For a while after my father died, household tasks seemed easier and no quarrels were worth pursuing and it appeared pointless to discuss future dates, even in casual conversation, even those of small personal relevance, such as the Olympics. To restructure one's consciousness so that precariousness tags everything... All lights and shapes change. Little is not held dear. The minimum that is good nature and the stupidity of ill nature: say this to a companion and you are uncompanionable. The answers will be delivered in the voice that educators develop for dealing with the bright-eyed slow and gradually extend to anyone however agreeable.

The awareness of a mortal state. When cliché reassumes its rare power and forces on you a truth that you can handle only in set phrases, communicate nothing. It is spitting into the sea.

XV

A female ghost of repeated weeping inhabits such nineteenth-century terraces as these. A coil of tears can unspring throughout the day in each untenanted room. Heat got into her useless bones, made her sorry of her limbs, melted her down Arethusa-like into mere flow of summer and never-again. The ghost rises earlier and earlier, doing less and less, an imagined embarrassment to the unseeing company who otherwise enjoy however little life there might be in her appallingly lengthened day.

There is silent crying, crying with murmurs, crying and snivelling, crying with involuntary whimpering, crying with jerking motions. Is there something sexual in the ghost's relief? Bodiless, she finds the nearest consolation: abandonment to spasms. Those who live in these houses share her spasms of the mind, shut down except to peer over the verge of a sorrow down which again and again to tumble.

The sky bright through ice-blue curtains, pattern name dot.com waterfall. The blasted birds sounding like fury. One city bombed. Another city threatened by a hurricane. The ghost is not getting through. The lights flicker at all hours in the windows across the street. I have not tried to make contact.

No lifting but what one can make out of this grief.

XVI

I would be taught to write by a writer. I would be taught to write by a writer who likes students who chase after his liking. The writer would not like me; not as a student. I would produce work for regular assessment. Writing does not take place in the locus of disappointment. Words do not lie low in silence, forming and re-forming, being taken out and letting in the sunnish blue. Being taught by a writer, I would be among other writers. Sharing a stall makes writers better. The young don tells me about a young don's sonnets that are beautifully controlled. The young don looks ill with admiration of a messy poem, before asking whether all the allusions had been meant. The young don could not translate 'lyrical castrates' back into the original language, and who ever dreamt up such a judgmental phrase? The young don giggles, looking helpful and undisturbed but for his attitude of fear before a true thing-that-is-not-to-be-encouraged. To have a task, and a method, and the need to know the non-writing world, is to make a claim on the property of aloneness. It was in the search for educators that the habits of holding back were learnt. I walk about two rooms in spills of exaltation, making no cents.

The trees in the park have been clipped artfully. They look wild. It is as if they just happen to have swept aside or dropped one of their own branches, avoided an angle or tilted their top to open another and another vista: plum foliage, spikes from harsher climates and thousand-year-plus traditions of scratching non-representative trees on rock or painting a leaf, with exactitude, on silk. The ground moves beneath the feet if the neck tips back. Bursts of yellow-green capture and contribute to the heightening of light. A man from another city, walking here, collided with a female student. Their eyes met. He knew she was The One. From her spiritual, creative look, he thought that she must be a student of English. Now the man was on a quest. Each weekend, he travelled from his home to this city, hunting his Beatrice. In the English Faculty buildings, he sought a photo board. He identified the college nearest the park. Impressed by his persistent entering of University buildings without permission, the college gave him access to their email lists. For was this not true love in the early twenty-first century? Fortunate the man not to have fallen in love with a bank clerk or estate agent! For who would have tolerated his quest had he tried to pursue it through such offices? The eagle claws of Barclays would have torn him. He would have been disdained by the dispensers of letting contracts. Fortunate the man not to be a goth, a punk, a Rastafarian, a black-toothed, straw-hatted, mountain-eyed guitarist leading a donkey, or anything other than pink-skinned and with a reasonable array of teeth! And fortunate the man to be a man! For who knows what his Beatrice did want, in her presumed state of wanting without knowing she wanted, but that surely she wanted a man?

This day begins late enough. The speaking voice wakes up so claggy. Read aloud a verse by someone else, to re-tune it? I could think only of Dante's stony poems, *pietrose*. I wanted to draw on their clunky power. Yet I did not desire to start the day with that scatter of yellow hair and ardour trapped in consonantal rocks – the movement being a little too slow, the impetuosity being that of a beast's snarl even as the metal-trapped leg trails behind. I desired again the marvellous impulse of the *Inferno*. All of a sudden this appeared to me as purely intellectual in its emotion. When the light, sinful beasts come leaping down towards the poet, they course as smoothly as the terza rima. They may be bad creatures within the poem, but they are written with, and move with, the ease and brilliance of a mind that has slipped its traces. The poet of the *Commedia* does not begin by putting on a yoke of religion or false habit of sublimation. The poetry itself is a freeing of the mind from obsession with a love-object, in that it can play to the uttermost in every intellectual system available to it. There is true emotion in the full engagement of the mind's powers.

So I have read nothing aloud. And this morning I have not been silent, nor read before anything else a good text, nor written one real thing here! I am sending this to you now, and hope that you will rewrite it; I love how you make the time.

Measures of Expatriation — VII

Syllable of Dolour

For the whole space that's in the tyrant's grasp,
And the rich East to boot.
– Shakespeare, *Macbeth* IV. iii.

my pretty ones
only go away
nor ask just
ice inwardly sutures
flow as flesh
glued old calabash
it hurts perspective
towns drowned fairs

see i'm small
in Tempo Peril
look back like
Psyche crying mountain
reversing into youth
laughter on the
please believe this
hypothermia naps cobalt

if you will
slalom heedless colourfast
i'm shy hell
boy crying wolf
head picked kicked
inside only where
the lake sunk
whisht non temere

Pobrecillo Tam

'Only I do not like the fashion of your garments. You will say they are
Persian attire, but let them be changed.'
– Shakespeare, *King Lear* III. vi.

raise yr gme said my friend lucky
in love since going online
to learn moves that lead from geek
to playa. go to the big
baldwin city; life's laid out like
yr sister's tea set that time
she spilled the milk & didn't
cry for a real melting knife.
chamoised my head & was going,
radiant as a hermit's cave
in cappadocia; fled Him
& my other dogs & wall-
papered my sister's braced smile
in carious photographs.
well caramel you can cross,
pass, shoot for the stars, scrape sky
for a living but don't hang
yr washing from the window –
the old man doesn't like it;
& see that tree? it translates
spring will bring again bread stone
scorpion to hand; always
afternoon if once you stand
in His light. i prayed for lift-off
& became a little horse
shadowed by an always car;
i prayed for inside, needed
shadow like a crown on my head,
lived off foods composed of sub-
stitutions. Lady of sit-
uations, i pray for lift-
off, tailoring my head & bust
to rise above this city
of unkadare nature,
pushkin types, fatalistic
pedestrians who're at the start
of my game, who're my true loves,
if only their hearts were Gabriel,
& not being borgesed to death
staying off the drive-by streets,
mummified in the seven
sealed orifices firstnamed home.

Sycorax ~~W~~hoops

'I' th' commonwealth I would, by contraries,
Execute all things [...]'
– Shakespeare, *The Tempest* II. i.

Mother! plague of angels in the house – thinkin stranglin,
oh shit, applied bakin soda remedies instead, witherin
final refrigerator angels cloggin language
like they'd free us from knowin it's true ~~further~~
Father Zeus airdrops party favours, fractures syntax,
gettin the glitter out of ~~war~~ where we're ~~struck~~ stuck livin,
sex ~~existin~~, plane to sea. Mother, our cities! ~~cold~~
called on Aphrodite, AIDS worker, to ~~blonde~~ bond us
again with ~~triage~~ ties of love. Maa! Thinkin writin.
Turned over a new leaf to indict ~~science~~ ~~silence~~
siloed ~~whiteness~~ witness; was a portal, no paper;
near as narnia, fell in; this ~~darling~~ darkling plain!
It's rainin in Ilium. There's somethin classic
about this situation which eye must not, nor heart,
articulate, though bearin it, we do, and have sung
songs whose vibration slips the mascara from those gods,
though a man lookin down on us dogs us with kind thoughts
he kind of attributes to us ~~as tributes to him~~.
Mother! plunge your tongue where ever with brokenness we're ~~deaf-~~
~~en'd~~ ~~defend~~ fed. Take ~~apart~~ our part. Launch in sighted
darkness our pack of languages, fluid as hounds,
all ready: bathed: riteful: already intending chase:

Un Furl

Any love
meant as equal
is momentary
momentarily unequal
is equal
if love
reckons time
knows not equals

Energy pie
cuts recurrent
numbers, finishes
sweet-and-sorry plates
Crumbs, dolcezza
defend the knife
nobody likes
for no body
likes it

Not 'I,
you or me,
Thou and I' –
This is
it, is
it and it
its itness
it's itness

Who decides
whose in-charge
electrifies what passing
belle of limits?
Recoup value
for re-cooped
available valuables?
Sacrifice this good,

Who decides?
Good, good
doesnae transfur;
disney compute:

faithful rewrites
'until death'
pandemic formula
various loveprosy
miss difference
in recognition
miss recognizable
in differentiate, shun

love's capitalists
worry: six
cats equivalent
one convent;
one man,
half a boat,
five wives
and two ghosts
unbalanced
if add
six-tenths person,
remembered and dismembered
trees, three
over two jobs,
sundry passports,
samurai, and pedestrianism?

A way of working
word for word
breath in breath
skin on skin
dream to dream
transfurrable skills
say let's
play with you

Stalker

for K. M. Grant

He waits. Without knowing me,
he waits. The tips of branches,
edible and winey, bring
spring by suggestion to him
who in autumn dawn, eager,
with wet knees, disregards me,
being drawn by me. He waits
and in me he waits. I branch,
the form is branching, it bounds
like sight from dark to bright, back
again. The form is from me:
it is him, poem, stag, first sight
and most known. In him I wait:
(when he falls) needs must (hot heap),
nothing left over (treelike
no longer) nor forlorn: we're
totalled.

Leila Capildeo and family; Katie Grant and household; Madre Marina Barbero (i.m.); Tracy Assing; Nadine Brooker; the Byragie Marajh family, and in honour of the memory and legacy of Pandit Kaysho; Pat Byrne; Madeleine Campbell; Theo Celot; Joan Dayal; Elspeth Duncan; Ian Duhig; Anthony Esposito; Giles Goodland; Revd Dr Peter Groves; Laura Guthrie; Lucy Hannah; Jeremy Hardingham; Katy Hastie; Susannah Herbert; Idara Hippolyte and family; Eve Lacey; Nicholas Laughlin; Maisie Lawrence; John Robert Lee; Vladimir Lucien; Agata Maslowska; Michael Mendis; Rod Mengham; Iain Morrison; Inge Milfull; Kei Miller; Metu Miller; Drew Milne; Ron Paste; Shivanee Ramlochan; Giselle Rampaul; Tanya Singh; Attillah Springer; Tanya Syed; Molly Vogel; Courtenay Williams; John Whale; Café Writers, Norwich; *Commonwealth Writers*, Commonwealth Foundation; Fruitmarket Gallery, Edinburgh; The Oratory of St Alphege, Southwark; Michael Schmidt, generous emperor.

IN PRINT

Cambridge Literary Review; *The Missing Slate*; *PN Review*; *Poetry & Audience*; *Prac Crit*; *Wasafir; Cybermohalla Hub* (Sarai-CSDS and Sternberg Press, 2012); *Disappearing Houses* (Vahni Capildeo and Andre Bagoo, Alice Yard, 2011); *Furies: A Poetry Anthology of Women Warriors* (forbookssake, 2014); *New Poetries VI* (Carcanet, 2015); *The Arts of Peace* (Two Rivers Press, 2014); *Gathered Here Today: Celebrating Geraldine Monk at 60* (Knives, Forks and Spoons, 2012).

ONLINE

a glimpse of; *Blackbox Manifold*; *Almost Island*; *Clinic*; *Gangway*; *Molly Bloom*; *Poetry and Pictures at the Museum*; *Shoes Or No Shoes?*; *Tender*; *Visual Verse*.